EL SALVADOR
A Revolution Confronts
The United States

Cynthia Arnson

Institute for Policy Studies
Transnational Institute

Washington, D.C. and Amsterdam

The Institute for Policy Studies is a nonpartisan research institute. The views expressed in this study are solely those of the author.

Published by the Institute for Policy Studies.

Copies of this book are available from the Institute for Policy Studies, 1901 Q Street, N.W., Washington D.C. 20009, or The Transnational Institute, Paulus Potterstraat 20, 1071DA, Amsterdam, The Netherlands.

First Printing, 1982
Second Printing, 1983

ISBN 0-89758-036-2

ACKNOWLEDGEMENTS

I wish to extend special thanks to Saul Landau and to Jorge Sol Castellanos, without whose suggestions, patience, and encouragement this work would not have appeared.

Space and discretion prevent me from naming all of the Salvadorans whose time and cooperation have been essential to this work. To them I extend a collective note of deep appreciation. Many U.S. officials have also extended their generous cooperation. I am also grateful to Heather Foote, Peggy Healy, Thomas Quigley, Rona Weitz, Reggie Norton, Cynthia Buhl, John Dinges, and Ed Killackey, from whom I have learned many important lessons about Central America.

Special thanks go to Martin Gonzalez, who assisted with initial research, and Jacqueline Sharkey, for her tremendous help in preparing the manuscript.

Finally, I wish to thank my colleagues at the Institute for Policy Studies who helped in innumerable ways, especially Carole Collins, Deborah Smith, Peter Kornbluh, Eliana Loveluck, Craig Nelson and Flora Montealegre.

C.A.
March 19, 1982

TABLE OF CONTENTS

iii

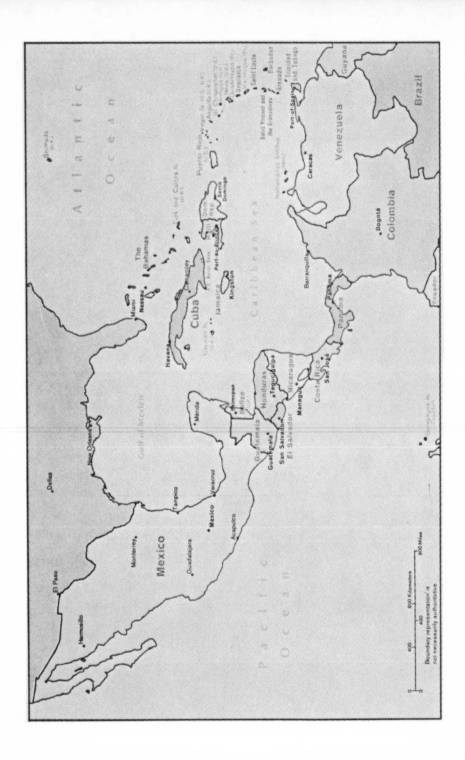

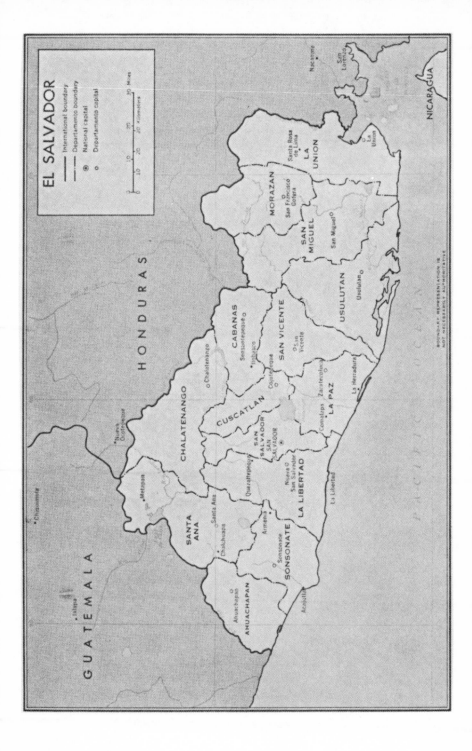

EL SALVADOR
— — — International boundary
———— Departamento boundary
⊛ National capital
○ Departamento capital

GUATEMALA

HONDURAS

NICARAGUA

PACIFIC OCEAN

BOUNDARY REPRESENTATION IS
NOT NECESSARILY AUTHORITATIVE

Chiquimula

Nueva
Ocotepeque

Metapan

SANTA
ANA

Santa Ana

Chalchuapa

Ahuachapan

AHUACHAPAN

Armenia

Sonsonate

SONSONATE

Acajutla

Quezaltepeque

Nueva
San Salvador

LA LIBERTAD

La Libertad

SAN
SALVADOR
SAN
SALVADOR

Chalatenango

CHALATENANGO

Sensuntepeque

CABANAS

Ilobasco

Cojutepeque

CUSCATLAN

Suchitoto

San
Vicente

SAN VICENTE

Zacatecoluca

Cojutepeque

LA PAZ

La Herradura

MORAZAN

San Francisco
Gotera

SAN
MIGUEL

San Miguel

USULUTAN

Usulutan

Santa Rosa
de Lima

LA
UNION

La
Union

San
Lorenzo

Nacaome

PROLOGUE

SAN SALVADOR — Men in uniform and civilian clothes drove into a poor suburb before dawn yesterday, pulled 23 people from their homes and shot them dead in the street, witnesses said. Seven more people were slain in their homes in front of their families. When reporters arrived in the suburb of Monte Carmelos, 23 bodies ripped by automatic weapons fire were strewn for 100 yards. Two homes were burned, apparently by fires started by bazooka rounds.

"It was the National Guard, and police," shouted several residents.

The street where the victims were slain ran with the blood and the victims, presumed to be leftist suspects, were disfigured by large-caliber slugs pumped into their heads and chests . . . .

— from wire reports, April 7, 1981

MOZOTE — The 15 houses on the main village street had been smashed. In two of them, as in the sacristy, the rubble was filled with bones. All of the buildings, including the three in which body parts could be seen, appeared to have been set on fire, and the remains of the people were as charred as the remaining beams . . . . The road was littered with animal corpses, cows and horses. In the corn-fields behind the houses were more bodies, those unburned by fire but baked by the sun. In one grouping in a clearing in a field were 10 bodies: two elderly people, two children, one infant—a bullet hole in the head—in the arms of a woman, and the rest adults . . . .

— *The Washington Post*, January 27, 1982

"North and South Vietnam had been, previous to colonization, two separate countries," said President Ronald Reagan at a February 17, 1982 press conference. The 1954 Geneva provisions, the president continued, stated that "these two countries could by a vote of all their people decide together whether they wanted to be one country or not." The president declared that the Vietnamese Communist leader Ho Chi Minh "refused to participate in such an election."[1]

President Reagan was wrong. Vietnam was one country before French colonial rule divided it into three states. The Geneva Accords, recognizing Vietnamese unity,   1 called for a temporary partition only—until the general elections scheduled for 1956. U.S.-installed South Vietnamese President Ngo Dinh Diem, not Ho Chi Minh, refused to participate in the elections. The question of unity was never debated. Diem himself publicly vowed to reunify Vietnam under his rule. When called on the gaffe, White House officials played down the importance of the president's error. "I don't think it's the heart of what really concerns people in this country," said David Gergen, the White House communications director.[2]

History, it has often been said, is written by the conquerors. President Reagan and his foreign policy team appear at times to have written it for their convenience. In 1981, the Reagan administration outlined its interpretation of recent Salvadoran history, in order to explain U.S. policy. ". . . Cuba, the Soviet Union, and other Communist states . . . are carrying out what is clearly shown to be a well-coordinated, covert effort to bring about the overthrow of El Salvador's established government and to impose in its place a Communist regime with no popular support."[3] In March 1982, Secretary of State Alexander Haig described the Salvadoran guerrilla movement as "the Marxist-Leninist extension of the Sandinista-Cuban-Soviet effort," and said that the guerrillas were "commanded, controlled, and run externally— completely."[4]

The United States showed scant interest in Vietnam until the 1950s; it ignored Salvadoran politics until 1979. Not that this was necessarily disadvantageous—El Salvador is one of the few Central American and Caribbean states that escaped landings by U.S. Marines or naval forces in the past 100 years. However, during the past three years, the United States has become increasingly involved with this nation. Like Vietnam, El Salvador and its internal strife are being cast in the spotlight of Cold War competition with the Soviet Union.*

Secretary of State Haig has said the United States will do "whatever is necessary"[5] to prevent El Salvador from falling into the hands of "Marxist-Leninists," as he has

---

* The original U.S. reason for involvement in Vietnam in the 1950s was to contain China.

labeled the Salvadoran opposition. A nation that previously had been given little official notice has now emerged as a focal point of U.S. policy.

Thus far, however, policy elites, many of whom have scant or no experience in Latin America, have shown little understanding of Salvadoran history, or of the organic links between that history and the current conflict. Reagan administration officials, moreover, have fired or transferred foreign service officers who disagree with the current policy approach, much as China experts were purged from the State Department in the early 1950s.

Politicians, journalists, and activists have drawn analogies between El Salvador and Vietnam, seeing in the administration's escalating support of the Salvadoran government and heated rhetoric a repeat of the experience that led to the landing of U.S. troops in Southeast Asia. Others have suggested different metaphors, or rejected the Vietnam analogy altogether.

Former U.S. Ambassador to El Salvador Robert White, for example, predicted that sending U.S. troops to El Salvador would be similar not to U.S. action in Vietnam, but to the Soviet intervention in Afghanistan. In the U.S. Congress, legislators in favor of a negotiated solution have drawn parallels between El Salvador and Zimbabwe, suggesting that a devastating guerrilla war can be brought to an end through internationally-sponsored negotiations.

Secretary of State Haig has also dismissed the Vietnam metaphor, saying that El Salvador, unlike Vietnam, is in an area truly vital to U.S. national security, and that "we are going to succeed and not flounder as we did in Vietnam."[6] The administration has become so determined to prevent a guerrilla victory that at times it seems to be ignoring both U.S. public opinion* and the advice of European allies.

However, abstractions about situations such as those in Vietnam, Afghanistan, Cuba and Zimbabwe—and the policies built around them—make little sense unless they

---

*According to a *Newsweek* poll conducted in late February 1982, 89% of Americans familiar with Reagan policy in El Salvador do not want the U.S. to send troops, 60% are against supplying military equipment, and 54% want the U.S. to keep its hands off altogether.[7]

are considered in a historical context. Solutions to complex problems must proceed from analysis rooted in an understanding of local political culture and historical processes: how did the conflict evolve in El Salvador? Why did it escalate, even after 1979, when a government that promised to break with the old order came to power? Who were the major actors and forces in this century that shaped the country's politics and oriented its economy? When has the United States expressed its interest in Salvadoran affairs, and what form did U.S. policy take? What will bring peace to El Salvador, and how can that be implemented?

In El Salvador, massacres such as the ones that occured in the Salvadoran suburb of Soyapango and in Mozote have become commonplace, carried out under the pretext of stopping Soviet-orchestrated terrorism. Between October 15, 1979 and December 1981, there were more than 30,000 politically motivated killings in the country.[8] Soyapango and Mozote, like My Lai a decade ago, may seem the quintessence of foreignness, but the American stake in El Salvador no longer permits it to be a forgotten republic somewhere south of the border.

INTRODUCTION

Central America has five republics, just as a hand, said Chilean poet Gabriela Mistral, has five fingers. Mistral called El Salvador the *pulgarcito*—the little thumb—because it is the smallest of the countries.

El Salvador is also the most densely populated, with about 4.5 million inhabitants in an area of about 8,400 square miles.[9] Sixty percent of the population lives in the countryside, where, until an attempt at land reform in 1980, 2 percent of Salvadorans owned 60 percent of the land.[10] El Salvador's per capita income is lower than that of any country in the Western Hemisphere except Haiti.

El Salvador, "The Saviour," was given its name by Spanish conquerors led by Pedro de Alvarado, who invaded from Mexico in 1524. It took the Spaniards until 1547 to subdue the rebellious Indian population, descendants of the Aztecs and the Mayas. To control and exploit the Indians, the *conquistadores* instituted forms of forced labor—*encomienda* and *repartimiento*—which obliged the Indians to give over part of the product of their labor as tribute to the Spanish crown.

Spaniards expanded the traditional Indian cultivation of balsam and cacao, and used these crops for trade within the colonies and with Spain.[11] The Spaniards also introduced cattle-raising to El Salvador. During this time, the Spanish crown permitted Indian communities to maintain their pre-conquest forms of communal land holding in the form of *ejidos* and tribal lands.*

In addition to agricultural products, the Spaniards also brought European diseases such as smallpox and syphilis to El Salvador. Although precise figures are not available, historians have estimated that the Indian population declined 80 percent in the first century after the conquest.[12] With land made available by the reduction in the Indian population, the Spaniards increased the cultivation of indigo for markets in Guatemala and

---

* See p. 11.

Europe, via Spain, on large *haciendas*. Until the end of the colonial period, two different forms of land use and ownership—private *haciendas* (including church property) and collective indigenous communities—predominated in El Salvador.

After Mexico declared its independence from Spain, Central America took advantage of the weakness of the crown, and declared its independence in 1821. It organized itself into a federation of five states—El Salvador, Guatemala, Honduras, Costa Rica, and Nicaragua—under the domination of Guatemala, the former seat of colonial administration. For approximately one year, Central America was annexed to the Mexican empire of Augustín de Iturbide. When Iturbide abdicated in 1823, Central America declared its absolute independence, and became the United Provinces of Central America.[13]

A series of wars followed independence from Spain and Mexico concerning the appropriate way to organize society and the state. Debates within the local merchant class over commercial policy and philosophy provided the underpinnings of the two principal political parties. Liberals, representing middle sectors that had been denied political and economic access under colonial rule, pressed for the liberalization of trade, the abandonment of clerical privilege, judicial reform, and republican forms of government. Conservatives, hopeful of regaining the monopolistic trading privileges of the colonial era, wanted a continuation of exclusive, royalist institutions. By 1829, the Liberals, led by Francisco Morazán, dominated the Central American federation. San Salvador, a Liberal stronghold, became its capital.

Beginning in 1825, Morazán began promoting private acquisition of Indian communal lands, a move that accelerated the concentration of land ownership in El Salvador and undermined traditional forms of land ownership. Peasant uprisings, which had not occured on a large scale since the conquest, began anew in 1832 under the leadership of Anastasio Aquino.[14] Disaffected Indians participated in the Conservative attempts to overthrow Morazán and the Liberal government. In 1839, the Conservatives triumphed, and Central America became a region of five separate republics under

6

Conservative rule.

Conservative control in El Salvador meant a return to Spanish colonial institutions, including the guarantees of communal forms of land ownership for the Indians. However, a tiny group of landholding families of Spanish descent—Regalado, Palomo, Escalón, Menéndez—limited access to and control of the political system to those who shared their wealth and status. In the mid-nineteenth century, they admitted into their ranks well-to-do European immigrants—Hill, Parker, Sol, D'Aubuisson, De Sola.[15]

The oligarchy used control of the government to further their own economic interests. When coffee cultivation was introduced to replace indigo production in the late 1800s, the oligarchy abolished Indian communal lands.

The political and economic relationships codified into laws in the nineteenth century remained intact into the twentieth.

When their economic power eroded during the Great Depression of the 1930s, El Salvador's oligarchy entrusted formal power to the military. From 1932 until 1979, El Salvador had only nine months of civilian rule. When industrialization and urbanization increased in the 1950s and 1960s, the agrarian-dominated economic structure of El Salvador changed to a degree, allowing for the formation of a middle class and a group of entrepreneurs, some of whom challenged the economic and political hold of the landed oligarchy and the military. Reformist political parties were organized, and labor and peasant unions were formed. But the ruling elite resisted all efforts to break its hold on El Salvador's economic and political system.

By the late 1970s, socio-economic indicators reflected the heritage of more than a century of oligarchic domination. Two-thirds of El Salvador's population received less than one-third of disposable income.[16] More than 50 percent of the country's peasants worked less than six months a year as wage labor on commercial plantations, and had almost no access to land—either through renting or sharecropping—in the off-season.[17] Between 1961 and 1975, the number of landless peasants grew from 11 percent to 40 percent of the rural

7

population.[18]

The political situation also reflected decades of military rule. Military officers considered normal forms of petition and protest illegal, and they brutally suppressed all forms of dissent. Groups representing sectors that were excluded from participating in the government— peasants, workers, students and some types of professionals—began choosing extra-systemic means to press their demands for better living conditions and access to the political arena. They occupied factories, seized land illegally, and staged peaceful sit-ins at foreign embassies. These activities were violently repressed by the armed forces. In turn, groups of armed guerrillas adopted violent means in an attempt to overthrow a government that refused to permit reform.

By October 15, 1979, the day of a coup by young reformist military officers, El Salvador was a polarized, fragmented society, with an economy still reliant on primary commodity exports at a time of soaring oil prices, inflation, and world recession. For more than 150 years, no foreign government had shown significant interest in its problems.

El Salvador became of interest to U.S. policymakers when societal breakdown raised the specter of leftist revolution. Throughout 1980, the Carter administration made a belated effort to promote reforms and curb official and extra-official violence. In 1981, the Reagan administration described the situation of open civil war in the country as a "textbook case of Communist aggression"[19] by the Soviet Union and Cuba. It undertook a rapid and massive expansion of military and economic aid to President José Napoleón Duarte, who was in power in alliance with the military. El Salvador, the *pulgarcito*, became the stage for the "decisive battle for Central America."[20]

THE SETTING

In the spring and summer of 1979, a group of Salvadoran colonels, majors and captains carefully watched the unfolding political-military situation in Nicaragua. Sandinista guerrillas, together with rag-tag bands of youths and citizens, appeared to be defeating dictator Anastasio Somoza's National Guard. On July 19, 1979, Somoza's army disbanded and fled in the wake of a popular uprising led by the Sandinistas. The group of Salvadoran officers learned two important lessons: that too much officially-sanctioned killing can produce revolutionary consequences, and that revolution meant the destruction of their military institution.

Wary of the repression and corruption that characterized the Salvadoran government of General Carlos Humberto Romero, these officers conspired to overthrow General Romero and his clique. They plotted in the San Carlos barracks in the capital and in the halls of the *Escuela Militar,* whose vice-director, Colonel Adolfo Arnoldo Majano, was to become one of the leaders of their movement. The officers were men in their thirties and forties, many of whom had been trained in the United States. Many of them believed in the legitimacy of popular demands for reform.

On October 15, 1979, less than three months after the Nicaraguan revolution had succeeded, they moved. General Romero fled to Guatemala with some of his senior officers; Colonel Majano and Colonel Jaime Abdul Gutiérrez, a former employee of El Salvador's telecommunications network ANTEL, took power on behalf of the Young Military Movement *(Movimiento de la Juventud Militar).* They turned to El Salvador's universities and opposition parties to form the country's first civilian-military junta in nearly twenty years.

State Department officials expressed relief. They had "encouraged"[21] the coup-leaders because it appeared that the officers would adhere to the U.S. rules for governing: initiate reforms while keeping the armed forces intact. For after the Nicaraguan revolution, U.S.

9

policymakers had become cognizant of the crisis in Central America, much as the Cuban revolution had shocked U.S. officials in 1959. In September 1979, one month before General Romero's overthrow, Assistant Secretary of State Viron Vaky had told Congress that "much of Central America is gripped by a polarizing dynamic for change, terrorism, and potential radicalization . . . the question is not whether change is to occur, but whether that change will be violent and revolutionary or peaceful and preserving of democratic values . . . ."[22] His prescription for El Salvador's problems, however, proved more cautious than his diagnosis: move up the elections General Romero had scheduled for 1982, and allow the return of political exiles.[23]

THE ROOTS OF THE CRISIS

El Salvador's crisis far pre-dated Washington's attention, however, and as the country's reformers soon learned, its roots proved deep and tenacious. They reach back into the nineteenth century, particularly the years 1879-1882, when coffee replaced indigo as El Salvador's main export.

Until that time, Spanish law and subsequent national legislation guaranteed communal lands for El Salvador's peasants. These comprised Indian tribal lands *(comunidades indigenas)* and large municipal land-holdings *(ejidos)* that were cultivated and passed down to succeeding generations and enabled the families inside a village or rural hamlet to be somewhat self-sufficient. The rapid expansion of large-scale coffee production put new demands on the system of land-use and tenancy that were incompatible with traditional land-holding patterns.

In 1879, President Rafael Zaldívar began to enact a series of laws that totally transformed the agrarian structure of El Salvador. On February 15, 1881, Zaldívar's government passed a decree abolishing communal lands, calling them "impediments to agricultural development . . . the circulation of wealth . . . and the independence of the individual."[24] On March 2, 1982, another decree abolished the *ejidos,* calling the "municipal institution . . . an obstacle for our agricultural development."[25] Like an accelerated enclosure movement, the new laws created for El Salvador a rural work force. Peasants could barely eke out an existence on tiny rented plots during the off-season and were forced to migrate to the coffee-growing regions during the time of harvest. In 1884, El Salvador's rulers created a police force to evict the rural population and force the peasants to work for coffee growers as low-paid wage earners.*²⁶

As a result of the abolition of communal lands and the expansion of coffee growing, El Salvador's economic structure was transformed into a plantation economy. Large tracts of the best farmland were owned by a few families, and were worked by cheap and abundant labor. Over the next forty years, the plantation economy was expanded to include sugar cane and cotton, but neither crop replaced coffee in importance.

As a result of the economic transformation, El Salvador's population, which had been growing at a slow rate since independence, increased dramatically, due to forced internal migration and the concentration of men and women workers in plantation centers. Since the 1880s, El Salvador's population doubled every twenty-five years;[30] even vast external migrations to other Central American countries and to the United States have not offset this growth, or the resulting demands on resources.

Coffee planters, Salvadorans of mostly European descent, formed an aristocracy that also controlled commerce and banking. The oligarchy did welcome foreign capital to build railroads, ports, and utilities; but it held onto the reins of national political and economic life. El Salvador possessed no substantial mineral deposits, and the winds on its Pacific Coast were too strong for banana cultivation. Without these traditional Central American inducements for outside capital, foreign investors stayed away.

Changes in government administration took place by agreements among small groups and families. The *Asociación Cafetalera*, founded in 1929, served as a kind of shadow government.[31] By 1931, wrote historian David Browning, "coffee was king .... It produced 95.5% of export earnings, paid the country's taxes, proportioned

---

* This led in 1889 to the creation of a mounted police force in the western coffee-growing departments of Ahuachapan, Sonsonate and Santa Ana.[27] In 1901, Salvadoran President Tomás Regalado brought in a Chilean military mission to direct the Salvadoran Army, formerly trained by French officers.[28] In 1912, President Manuel Araujo invited a Spanish Civil Guard officer to form El Salvador's National Guard out of the rural militias.[29]

funds for central and local government, financed the construction of roads, ports, and railroads, created permanent or seasonal employment for one part of the population and made the fortunes of a few."[32]

The Coffee Crash . . . and the *matanza*

"From the people with whom I talked I learned that roughly ninety percent of the wealth of the country is held by about one half of one percent of the population. Thirty or forty families own nearly everything in the country. They live in almost regal splendor with many attendants, send their children to Europe or the United States to be educated, and spend money lavishly (on themselves). The rest of the population has practically nothing . . . A socialistic or communistic revolution in El Salvador may be delayed for several years, ten or even twenty, but when it comes it will be a bloody one."

Major A. R. Harris
U.S. military attache
for Central American Affairs, 1931.[33]

The years 1929-31 marked the end of El Salvador's golden age of coffee; worldwide depression sent coffee prices spiralling downward, putting thousands of peasants out of work and straining the fortunes of the rich. Labor unrest grew, opening the way for rural union organizers, many of whom were socialists. On May Day, 1930, eighty thousand workers marched through San Salvador demanding an end to unemployment, a minimum wage for agricultural workers, and better working conditions in the countryside.[34]

The year 1930 also marked the return to El Salvador of Augustín Farabundo Martí. The son of a landowner, Martí was a student organizer and charter member of the Central American Socialist Party, founded in 1925. In El Salvador, he headed the *Socorro Rojo Internacional*, described in one of its leaflets as "a vast organization, without party affiliation, which accepts the idea of class struggle. It proposes to defend all the workers who are persecuted by imperialism, capitalist governments, and all other agencies of oppression . . . proportioning its legal aid and material and moral support to workers and their

13

families ... ."[35] In March 1930, Martí founded the Salvadoran Communist Party.[36]

In the late 1920s, Martí had directed his attention to struggles elsewhere in Central America. In 1928 he went to Nicaragua's Segovia mountains to fight alongside Augusto César Sandino, who was leading a guerrilla band against U.S. Marines who had occupied Nicaragua since 1912. Martí wrote to a friend that he hoped "the joint action of all the oppressed people of the continent will sweep away the last vestiges of Yankee imperialism."[37]

The El Salvador that Martí returned to in 1930 was wracked by violence and unrest. During the summer, the government of Pio Romero Bosque outlawed workers' strikes and the circulation of leftist leaflets, while the police, National Guard, and Army imprisoned hundreds for opposition activities. The government called for the national elections constitutionally scheduled for 1931. They were won by Arturo Araujo, a wealthy landowner married to an Englishwoman, who made a populist appeal to workers and promised a minimum standard of housing, health, education and wages for all Salvadorans. When Araujo took over the Presidency, he had the support of important sectors of the labor movement.[38]

Araujo's administration could not make good on its promises, however. The depression worsened in 1931 and peasants' demands for land reform went unmet. In the middle of the year, major peasant strikes were violently suppressed by Araujo's Vice-President and Minister of War, Maximiliano Hernández Martínez.* In December 1931, Hernández Martínez and his military clique staged a coup. Farabundo Martí and other leaders decided the time was right for an armed revolt, and set January 22, 1932, as the date.

The result of that ill-fated uprising has been well-chronicled;[40] its memory is a national trauma that haunted political struggles for decades. Poorly armed and poorly organized rebels in western El Salvador killed several hundred people, including local officials and

---

* A committed theosophist, Hernández Martínez believed in reincarnation. Hence, he said, "it is a greater crime to kill an ant than a man, because the man is born again at death, while the ant dies forever."[39]

members of the elite. Hernández Martínez and his troops retaliated by murdering between 10,000 and 30,000 people while putting down the revolt and then carrying out mass reprisals. The leader of the uprising, Farabundo Martí, was executed by firing squad.

The military remained in power for the next fifty years, convinced that repression was the best guarantor of social order in times of crisis. The oligarchy acceded to the generals, satisfied that its interests would be taken care of. Both the military and the oligarchy were determined that "communist agitation" would never again be allowed to disrupt the social fabric of El Salvador.

The alliance between the coffee oligarchy and the Army flourished during the first years of the Martínez regime. The general passed vagrancy laws designed to provide *latifundia* with a reliable source of cheap labor, outlawed peasant unions, and organized state banks and trading companies to finance and market coffee. The government discouraged industrial development. It was determined that nothing should displace the coffee, sugar and cotton sectors, and placed limits on the level of capitalization for many industries.[41] Martínez's rule was arbitrary and brutal. In the 1930s, he proclaimed his admiration for Benito Mussolini and Adolf Hitler.

Hernández Martínez's policies, however, grew more anachronistic as the 1930s progressed. In part, this resulted from changes in the United States' outlook: the Good Neighbor Policy of the Roosevelt Administration coincided with a desire to expand U.S. exports and investment in Latin America—a policy that clashed head on with Martínez's anti-industrial stance. Even more important, however, were changes inside El Salvador. A new middle class of professionals and government employees pressed for greater opportunities to participate in political life. A new sector of the Army saw industrialization as a way to modernize the economy and increase its control over national affairs.

By the early 1940s, international events resulting from World War II brought the contradictions of Martínez's rule into sharp focus. He joined the United States in declaring war on the Axis, despite his announced preference for fascist forms of government. Under pressure from the United States, Martínez cooperated   15 with the inter-American defense effort. He accepted the principles outlined in the Atlantic Charter, which included a clause on political freedom. But he continued to rule El Salvador with an iron hand and, in 1944, convened a Constitutional Assembly that elected him for an unprecendented fourth term.

On April 2, 1944, a group of young Army officers, frustrated in their own military careers and contemptuous of the personalism of Martínez's regime, initiated a coup. Martínez and troops loyal to him at first crushed the revolt, sending most participants before a firing squad. Soon, however, government and bank employees, supported by students and intellectuals, organized a general strike that crippled the capital. On May 8, Martínez resigned and fled the country.

General Andres Menéndez, Martínez's Minister of Defense, took over, invited some members of the opposition to join the government, and promised to hold free elections. But as the campaign got under way, pro-Martínez sectors of the Army and the oligarchy grew wary of the popularity—and chances of success—of Social Democratic Arturo Romero, a leader of the April uprising against Martínez and candidate for the presidency. Rather than run the risk of a victory by Romero, the Army staged a coup against Menéndez. The elections were never held, and Colonel Osmin Aguirre, chief of police and a leading participant in the 1932 massacre, took over. After rigged elections, General Salvador Castañeda became president. Political parties and labor organizations were dissolved, and their leaders killed or sent into exile.

For the next four years, political opposition in El Salvador was limited to competing factions of the Army.[42] But events in neighboring Guatemala, where Juan José Arevalo and Jacobo Arbenz were successfully presiding over a government committed to social reforms, provided continuing inspiration to the democratic movement in El Salvador. Sensing that similar currents were growing stronger in El Salvador, a group of young military officers, led by Major Oscar Osorio, overthrew the Castañeda government in 1948. Osorio and another officer joined two civilians in a new ruling Directorate. Osorio became president in 1950.

The 1950s: Internal Reform and Development

"Major Oscar Osorio, later to be a colonel, began a six-year term in 1950 ... The economy was booming. The coffee planters were sending their families to Europe and they themselves were buying Cadillacs like Texans. It was around this time the description of El Salvador as 'the world's smallest Texas' began making the rounds. This little joke was a source of irritation to the 'haves,' but the 'have nots' were not interested , never having heard of Texas."

Paul P. Kennedy
The Middle Beat, 1971. [43]

After Osorio took power, the era of "reformism" began in El Salvador, led by a new group of Army officers, government technocrats, and entrepreneurs attempting to industrialize the country. Riding the wave of a coffee boom in the late 1940s and early 1950s—revenues from coffee quadrupled during this time[44]—the government increased taxes on landowners and channeled resources into infrastructure projects—dams, hydroelectric plants, and ports—as well as agricultural and industrial ventures. The number of state institutions devoted to fostering industrialization expanded rapidly, as did the size of the government bureaucracy. Industrialization appeared to be the wave of the Salvadoran future.

The implications of this expansion were numerous. Foreign investment, especially from the United States, began to trickle in, in accordance with the Salvadoran government's plan to produce locally what had formerly been imported. An urban workforce developed, and was allowed to form labor unions. But the limits to modernization and the relaxation of political restrictions soon became evident. The military had no intention of turning power over to civilians, and in 1950 created the instrument—an official party—through which it would dominate politics for the next three decades. (The name of the official party, the Revolutionary Party of Democratic Unification—PRUD—was changed in 1962 to the Party of National Conciliation—PCN.) Industrialization, moreover, accelerated the concentration of wealth in El Salvador, as landowners used the surpluses generated by high coffee prices to participate in El Salvador's industrial boom.

Although El Salvador's economy began to diversify in the 1950s, several impediments to self-sustained growth remained. The major impediment was the lack of an internal market, which resulted from the concentration of wealth in the hands of a few families, and the subsistence-level existence of the peasantry. The situation had one obvious remedy—agrarian reform—which would have raised incomes for tens of thousands of people and expanded local demand.[45] The fact that agrarian reform did not accompany attempts at industrial expansion was evidence of the continued strength of the landed oligarchy, which had acceded to and participated in the industrial boom, rather than be displaced by it.

Thus, wrote historian Stephen Webre, "sixteen years after the fall of the dictator Martínez, arbitrary violence and repression remained characteristic of Salvadoran politics. A single, official party ruled the country, and all other political organizations existed and operated under conditions subject to the caprice of its leaders . . . when its opponents became too vociferous, the ruling party denounced them as Communists or reactionaries and called upon the support of the church hierarchy in its campaign against them. When they took to the streets, it loosed the police upon them . . . the primary weakness of this system . . . was its absolute dependence upon the Army . . . ."[46]

The Rise of Rivera

Two events in the late 1950s opened a new phase in Salvadoran politics, one marked by the search for an opportunity to establish a more democratic government and undertake socio-economic reforms. The first event was external, the Cuban revolution in 1959; the second was internal and external, a dramatic decline in coffee prices in 1958,[47] which led to growing unrest among the rural population, as well as rising prices and unemployment. Both factors convinced officers around incumbent president José María Lemus that changes—

however modest—might be needed to forestall social upheaval.

In October 1960, a coup deposed the Lemus regime. In retrospect, the period appears as a kind of dress rehearsal for events 19 years later. Junior officers responsible for the coup formed a junta, inviting prominent liberal civilians affiliated with the university to join them. They promised a return to order and constitutional government, and free elections. But they stressed the transitional nature of their government, and avoided announcing broad social and economic reforms. Nonetheless, the business sector decried the new government as "communistic," and for several months the United States withheld recognition.[48]

The October coup resulted in few changes, but unleashed a flood of activity. Students and workers took to the streets demanding a minimum wage, new labor laws, and agrarian reform. Important sectors of the Army, however, became wary of the intense activity, and grew suspicious of civilian reformers in their midst who expressed sympathy for the Cuban revolution. Four months after the coup, another group of officers overturned the civilian-military junta. Lieutenant Colonel Julio Rivera and Colonel Aníbal Portillo declared their government would be anti-Cuban, anti-Castro, and anti-communist,[49] and they selected a less militant group of civilians to govern at their side.

The Alliance for Progress

The coup leaders basked in Washington's approval. President John F. Kennedy, also fearful of Castro's example, had just announced the Alliance for Progress, designed to alleviate revolutionary symptoms in Latin America with the twin remedies of social reform and counterinsurgency. "Governments of the civil-military type of El Salvador are the most effective in containing communist penetration in Latin America," Kennedy said shortly after Rivera took office.[50]

In 1961 alone, the United States provided $25 million in loans to the new government.[51] Portraits of Kennedy and

Abraham Lincoln hung in Colonel Rivera's office.[52]

"Economic development" became one of the catchphrases of the Alliance for Progress; its logic held that new opportunities for the poor would reduce social grievances and the appeal of calls for revolutionary change. Moreover, it was thought that economic growth would create an expanding middle class, which was seen as the bastion of liberal democratic values.

In 1961, with Washington's support, five Central American republics formed the Central American Common Market, a plan for regional economic integration to expand trade and internal markets. The benefits to El Salvador were substantial: economic integration could forestall the need for sweeping internal changes, especially agrarian reform.[53]

More than half of all foreign investment in El Salvador since the turn of the century was made in the 1960s; between 1950 and 1967, for example, the book value of U.S. investment in El Salvador rose from $19.4 million to $45 million.[54] The country had so many light manufacturing industries which produced paint and paper products, processed foods, wire and light bulbs, that El Salvador became known as the "Ruhr of Central America."[55] New markets for Salvadoran industrial products were found in lesser-developed Honduras and Nicaragua. Between 1961 and 1968, the volume of intraregional trade grew 32 percent annually.[56]

A second facet of the Alliance for Progress, one closely related to the goal of economic development, brought teams of U.S. military advisers in closer contact with their Salvadoran counterparts. To provide the stability and internal security that would allow economic development to flourish, the United States initiated military and police aid programs to "professionalize" the armed forces and enhance their ability to combat Castro-style guerrillas. Although no guerrilla movements existed in El Salvador, these measures were seen as "preventive medicine." During the 1960s, the United States reorganized the police school, and trained and equipped riot control units in the National Police and National Guard. The Agency for International Development's Office of Public Safety established a central police records bureau in El Salvador, and installed a teletype system linking the Central American countries.[57] The network included entries on "suspected subversives."[58] By 1967, AID analysts concluded that U.S. public safety advisers had "efficiently trained the National Guard and National Police in basic tactics so that authorities have been successful in handling any politically-motivated demonstrations in recent years."[59]

As U.S. officials had hoped, economic expansion in El Salvador resulted in the formation of centrist political parties. The most important, the Christian Democratic Party (PDC), was founded in 1960; it enjoyed rapid, spectacular success in local elections. By 1964, the Christian Democrats had won the election for mayor of San Salvador, an office they would hold until 1976. By 1968, nearly half the deputies in the National Assembly represented opposition parties.[60]

The U.S. government, and especially the U.S. Ambassador to El Salvador, Murat W. Williams, put pressure on the Rivera government to comply with the aims of the Alliance for Progress. The government raised income taxes and adopted an electoral reform that did away with the "winner take all" provisions for the majority party in favor of proportional representation in the National Assembly and municipal councils, based on electoral returns. For his advocacy of agrarian reform, however, Williams earned the emnity of the oligarchy, who protested the "punitive nature" of his proposals and on numerous occasions snubbed the ambassador in public.[61] Williams also came into conflict with U.S. military representatives stationed in the Embassy and at the Pentagon when he urged that the size of the U.S. military mission be drastically cut. "Alas," said Williams, "the changes were all set back when Kennedy died and President Johnson made Tom Mann Assistant Secretary of State. Mann insisted that we must stay close to the oligarchy and the Army because they had the power."[62]

In the absence of agrarian reform, the crisis in the countryside worsened. El Salvador's population had doubled between 1931 and 1961,[63] as did the population in the capital, but new jobs in the industrial sector were limited. For a while, pressures in the countryside were eased by vast migrations of Salvadorans, many of whom crossed the northern border into Honduras and set up

21

squatters' and farm communities. It was estimated that as many as 300,000 Salvadorans had emigrated to Honduras by the late 1960s.[64] The Salvadorans were resented by the Honduran peasants, who regarded them as competitors for jobs and scarce resources.

The Hondurans' resentment was exacerbated by policies of the Central American Common Market. The Honduran government had joined with Nicaragua in protesting the arrangements of the Common Market, which relegated the region's least industrialized economies to the role of importers of foreign products.

In 1969, the Honduran government, pressed by an organized *campesino* movement, renewed its land reform effort. The government confiscated tracts held by Salvadorans, forcing thousands to return to their homeland. Nationalist feelings in both countries flared. The result was a six-day war, which El Salvador won. The Salvadoran Army occupied hundreds of square kilometers of Honduran territory until forced to withdraw by the Organization of American States. Before their retreat, Salvadoran soldiers looted stores, homes, and churches, earning the resentment of broad sectors of the Honduran population.

As a result of the war, Honduras broke off economic relations with El Salvador. El Salvador's share of the Honduran market was absorbed by Guatemala, and El Salvador's trade with the rest of Central America was impaired by its lack of access to Honduran highways. Although trade among members of the Central American Common Market continued to increase, El Salvador lost its advantageous position.

Inside El Salvador, however, the victory contributed to a wave of nationalism that benefitted the military. Combatants became war heroes; focus was temporarily shifted from internal problems. Riding a crest of enthusiasm, the official party of the military regained control of a number of cities and towns in local elections in 1970. The Christian Democrats, who had controlled 78 municipalities in 1968, lost all but eight in 1970.[65] They charged electoral fraud, but pro-government newspapers in the capital surmised that in the wake of war, only the party of the military could guarantee national security.

The Christian Democrats began to regroup. They took a lesson from the victory of Salvador Allende's *Unidad Popular* over the Christian Democrats in Chile and began to realize that coalition politics might be the way to national power.[66]

THE 1970s:
BITTER CHALLENGES

"As we look into the future, it is hard to see how El Salvador can compete for many decades in the world export markets with these particular crops (coffee, cotton, and sugar) unless people are willing to keep plantation wages low . . . . Already the three products are in world oversupply, with downward price tendencies."

David R. Raynolds
Rapid Development in Small Economies:
The Example of El Salvador, 1967.[67]

The weakening of El Salvador's position in the Central American Common Market and an accompanying fall in coffee prices in 1969 sent the Salvadoran economy into a tailspin. Immigrants to Honduras returned *en masse,* further straining limited land resources, and Salvadoran industry reeled from the loss of its lucrative Honduran market. Between 1970 and 1974, per capita income in El Salvador fell 2.6 percent annually.[68] El Salvador's balance of trade position worsened considerably as shrinking industrial exports failed to keep pace with soaring oil prices set by the Organization of Petroleum Exporting Countries.

International factors contributed to economic crises in all Third World countries in the 1970s, but El Salvador's were exacerbated by internal political events. With economic conditions no longer favoring flirtations with democracy and "limited openings," the Salvadoran Army moved against its opponents, defrauding civilian candidates out of national electoral victories and repressing the activities of opposition organizations. However, these reprisals no longer were met with the passivity of a peasant population haunted by the memories of 1932. Progressive Catholic clergy, spurred by the mandate of the 1968 Bishops' Conference in Medellín, Colombia, worked with El Salvador's rural poor to defend social and economic rights. Salvadoran labor unions, which had operated under government restrictions since the 1950s, resisted the effects of a faltering economy by intensifying bread-and-butter demands. University

24

students joined in the countercultural movement of the 1970s, adopting new life styles and openly proclaiming that their heroes were Karl Marx, Mao Tse-Tung, and Che Guevara. The Salvadoran military and the oligarchy could no longer count on a resilient economy to buy off unrest. The measures they chose—widespread violence against what they defined as the sources of subversion—further undermined the legitimacy of their rule. The decade of the 1970s marked the breakdown of El Salvador's political order.

The Electoral Fraud of 1972

In September 1971, the Christian Democrats and two smaller parties—the National Revolutionary Movement (MNR) and the National Democratic Union (UDN)—came to an agreement. As El Salvador's preeminent democratic forces, they decided to bury political differences, combine their strengths, and organize a joint bid for their presidency in 1972. They called their coalition the National Opposition Union (UNO). They nominated José Napoleón Duarte, the charismatic former mayor of San Salvador and a Christian Democrat, as their candidate for president, and chose Guillermo Ungo, a Social Democrat, as their candidate for vice-president. Duarte and Ungo campaigned vigorously throughout the country, basing their platform on agrarian reform and the restoration of democratic freedoms. They called the oligarchy and imperialism "the two faces of the hateful coin of dependency."[69]

The incumbent president of El Salvador, Fidel Sánchez Hernández named the official party's candidate. Sánchez Hernández selected his personal secretary, Colonel Arturo Armando Molina, who toured the country by helicopter[70] and repeated the PCN's long-unfilled promises regarding solutions to economic problems. The oligarchy looked even further to the right for a candidate to guarantee their interests. They found him in General José Alberto Medrano, former head of the National Guard. Medrano headed a conservative splinter of the official   25 party called the United Independent Democratic Front (FUDI) and chose as his vice-presidential running mate Raúl Salaverría, a representative of one of El Salvador's wealthiest coffee families.

The presidential campaign of 1971-72 marked an almost unprecedented mobilization of the Salvadoran populace. Duarte and Ungo visited more than two hundred towns, capitalizing on opposition parties' political victories in local administrations throughout the countryside in the 1960s. They were viewed as geniune reformers, whose anti-oligarchic programs would mean economic and social improvements for El Salvador's majority. The ruling elite and their military allies became concerned. Announcements paid for by the oligarchy appeared in the national press portraying Duarte and Ungo as the puppets of communism. Two months before the election, an assassination attempt against Duarte narrowly failed; his driver was shot and killed. An official investigation produced no suspects, and the case was dropped.[71]

Sensing the opposition's popularity, the Sánchez Hernández administration began to take preemptive measures. Several days before the election, UNO's legislative candidates were removed from the ballots in six major departments of the country. Early election returns showed Molina ahead; then came the results from El Salvador's larger cities. Duarte defeated Molina 2 to 1 in the Department of San Salvador, and a similar trend was emerging in other areas. Suddenly El Salvador's radio and television stations ceased reporting the election results. The London *Economist* drily noted how "coincidental . . . that the government's position began to improve only when the results stopped being announced . . . ."[72] After a night of secret counting, the Central Elections Council announced that Molina had won 314,000 to 292,000.[73] Duarte and Ungo were enraged; even the Election Board of San Salvador charged that the Central Elections Council had changed the vote tally in the area of the capital. On February 25, 1972, the Legislative Assembly, with 31 deputies of the official party and one from the opposition, declared Molina the winner.

UNO leaders condemned the fraud, but the real

challenge to Molina's victory came from other quarters. On March 25, 1972, Colonel Benjamin Mejía, decrying the anti-constitutional character of the military government, called on junior officers to organize a movement to reestablish democratic institutions and freedoms. The Mejía revolt was crushed, however, as the Salvadoran Air Force, aided by planes from Nicaragua and Honduras, dropped bombs on the capital, and security forces came to the defense of the regime. Duarte was arrested and beaten, then exiled to Venezuela. Moderate politicians of the center shrunk back in bewildered disarray.

Beyond Electoral Politics—The Rise of the Left

The electoral fraud of 1972 was a watershed in Salvadoran politics: centrist and progressive civilian politicians had mounted a successful electoral bid for national power, only to have victory taken from them by the party of the generals. It was not the first, nor the last time the military resorted to fraud to deprive civilians of office. But the year is a landmark, because the 1972 elections accelerated the radicalization of groups that previously had been encouraged to participate in the political system. For peasants, slum dwellers, students, and workers, the vote became a mockery, something tolerated as long as it did not upset the traditional exercise of military power. Not only did the 1972 elections underscore the illegitimacy of generals *cum* presidents, they called into question the entire process for achieving democratization.

Political parties of the center and center-left did not abandon elections as a method to produce social change for several years. But they could no longer count on the support of their rank-and-file to endorse what many now viewed as an exercise in futility. Into the political vacuum moved a plethora of "popular organizations" and guerrilla groups with a more radical vision of what was necessary to change Salvadoran society, and a willingness   27 to use extra-systemic means—land seizures, occupations, strikes, and armed confrontation—to achieve that transformation.

Perhaps no institution in El Salvador in the 1960s and 1970s had as profound an impact on the country's social and political fabric as the Catholic Church. Once a pillar of the oligarchic system, itself a partaker of wealth and privilege, the official Church in Latin America in the 1960s began to define the poverty and oppression of the masses as a sin, "*the* most profound contradiction to Christian faith."[74] While many in the Church hierarchy maintained their allegiance to the existing order, scores of priests, nuns, lay workers, and catechists throughout the countryside and urban slums focused their work on the social, economic, and political conditions that reflected the "suffering features of Christ the Lord."[75] The Church's evangelizing mission, as redefined by the second Conference of Latin American Bishops in Puebla, Mexico in 1978, involved taking a "preferential option for the poor."[76]

In the 1960s in El Salvador, progressive Catholic clergy as well as members of the Christian Democratic Party defied official government bans and encouraged the formation of peasant leagues and federations. In 1965 the Christian Federation of Salvadoran Peasants (FECCAS) was organized, basing its demands on the issues of farmworkers' salaries and access to land and credit. The Church started literacy classes among the poor and fostered the creation of grassroots Christian communities (*Comunidades Eclesiales de Base*), groups which discussed concrete daily problems in light of biblical teaching. It sought to encourage peasants to become "active agents of change to seek such fundamental conquests as unions and the defense of labor rights."[77] The Church also sponsored "*Jornadas de Vida Campesina,*"during which urban-based students went to the countryside to experience peasant life. Young, middle-class people came away sensitized, often radicalized, by their first contact with rural misery.

The result of these activities among the poor, explained a Salvadoran priest in the 1970s, was that "little by little the peasants were overcoming fatalism. They were gradually beginning to understand that their situation of hunger and sickness, the premature death of many of their children, their unemployment, the verbal contracts for work that were never respected, that all these disasters are not due to the will of God but to the lust for profit of a few Salvadorans and to the peasants' passivity."[78]

These changes in consciousness and organization were not lost on the oligarchy or the military. Priests were labeled subversives and Communists, and they, along with peasant leaders, were arrested, tortured, and made to "disappear." In 1968, the head of the National Guard, General José Alberto Medrano, created a counterinsurgency force to operate in rural areas. It was called ORDEN (*Organización Democrática Nacionalista*, whose acronym is Spanish for order), a paramilitary spy network "to make a barrier to the attempts of the communists to provoke subversion in the countryside."[79] U.S. intelligence officials provided assistance to Medrano.[80] ORDEN counted on fear and misery to divide the rural population. It provided small rewards, favors, or protection in exchange for collaboration. Polarization in the countryside accelerated.

The Armed Left

In the early 1960s, following the example of Fidel Castro in Cuba, the Salvadoran Communist Party (PC) attempted to form guerrilla units to fight the regime. But the industrial expansion fostered by the Alliance for Progress and the Central American Common Market, along with the "democratic opening" of those years and the rise of middle-class political parties, doomed the effort. In the 1970s, however, widespread disillusionment with political processes coupled with a sharp economic downturn provided the climate for more radical approaches to change. In the first half of the decade, three important guerrilla groups emerged that were committed to the overthrow of the regime and the organization of a revolutionary party to achieve basic socio-economic and political transformations.

The first group that was organized, the Popular Forces of Liberation (FPL), was formed in the wake of a disagreement within the Communist Party over the issue of armed struggle. Frustrated with the cautious, electoral strategy of the PC and convinced that class conflict in El Salvador had reached a new level, Salvador Cayetano Carpio, then-Secretary General of the PC, led a group of union leaders, workers, and students out of the party and founded the FPL in April 1970.[81] The group initially comprised teachers, workers, and students. In 1974, it began serious efforts to organize the peasants, who provided the foundation for its later strength.

The FPL adopted the Chinese concept of "prolonged popular war," a combination of political work at the grassroots level with the formation of a guerrilla army and support network to wage a war of attrition against the government.

In 1971, radicalized students and intellectuals founded the People's Revolutionary Army (ERP). Unlike the FPL, the ERP held a short-term view of the revolutionary struggle, seeing the use of guerrilla military action as a means of inciting popular rebellion. However, its leaders admitted that this strategy isolated the guerrillas from the population. Only in 1977 did the ERP form its affiliated political party, the Salvadoran Revolutionary Party (PRS), to build direct links with the civilian population.[82]

The early "militarismo"—bombings, kidnappings, assassinations—of the ERP created other problems within the organization: personal ambition, fractionalism, and a lack of democratic procedures for carrying out party affairs. In 1975, one wing of the organization, in an attempt to impose its "hegemony" over other factions, accused ERP poet Roque Dalton of being a "Soviet-Cuban-CIA agent." After a mock trial, Dalton was executed. Two ERP leaders, Ernesto Jovel and Fermán Cienfuegos, left the organization in protest. Along with their followers, they founded the Armed Forces of National Resistance (FARN) in 1975.

The FARN shared the ERP's emphasis on mass insurrection, but more than the other guerrilla groups, it stressed the need for a broad class alliance that would also include "honest sectors" of the armed forces in the struggle for a democratic and revolutionary government.[83] The FARN initially had an urban base, and made its greatest inroads into the labor movement.

Throughout the 1970s, the armed groups of the left carried out assaults on government outposts and convoys, and killings—called *"ajusticimientos"* or "bringing to justice"—of informants and government sympathizers. They financed these activities by kidnapping and ransoming government officials and wealthy businessmen. Their numbers remained small, perhaps several hundred, but the military used unprecedented terror tactics to eliminate "subversion."

The Challenge Grows

"Frequently," observed the Mayor of San Salvador, José Antonio Morales Ehrlich in 1977, "hundreds of armed security personnel will occupy a given city, village, or agricultural area, searching all houses and taking into custody hundreds of innocent persons .... The purpose of these operations is not crime prevention, but rather to instill terror in the population as a whole. In this way people come to accept the violation of their human rights as something inevitable, a force that cannot be resisted .... "[84] Typical of the military's repression were events such as those in San Vicente in 1974; shortly after the founding of the Union of Rural Workers (UTC), National Guardsmen attacked the town of La Cayetana, where peasant villagers were engaged in a land dispute with a local *hacienda* owner. Six peasants were killed and another twenty made to "disappear" as troops raided homes, stealing food and money. The Catholic Bishops Conference demanded an investigation, but the initiative was stifled in a national legislature controlled by the official party.[85]

The incident in La Cayetana, however, deepened the schism between Church and the State. The bishop of San Vicente, Pedro Arnoldo Aparicio, excommunicated the National Guardsmen believed to be responsible for the incident. Archbishop Luis Chávez y González issued a pastoral letter calling for agrarian reform and reaffirming peasants' rights to mobilize.

The Salvadoran official personally responsible for ordering the massacre at La Cayetana was Molina's Minister of Defense, General Carlos Humberto Romero.[86] He was already well-known to students and intellectuals for his direction of the occupation of the campus of the National University in 1972. Approximately 800 students, professors and administrators were arrested. Romero enhanced his reputation for brutality in 1975, when he ordered troops to attack a peaceful student demonstration in San Salvador. Students were staging a solidarity march for their counterparts in Santa Ana who had occupied the local campus to protest government expenditures of $3.1 million to stage the Miss Universe pageant. Scores of students were wounded and killed during the San Salvador march, and more than 24 disappeared.*[87]

Although tensions increased in the early 1970s, the center and center-left parties did not abandon their attempts to take power through elections. Each time, however, the frauds became more blatant: in the 1974 municipal and legislative elections, for example, the government did not even bother to publish the results. By 1976 the UNO coalition that had campaigned in 1972 refused to participate in local elections after the electoral boards disqualified more than two thirds of their slates.+[88]

The effect of these scandals was to further erode the credibility of the electoral opposition. Indeed, it was the occasion of the 1974 local elections that resulted in formation of El Salvador's first mass-based popular coalition, the United Popular Action Front (FAPU). "There was no unity outside the electoral camp," said one of

---

* Groups immediately occupied San Salvador's Metropolitan Cathedral in protest, using the occasion to announce the formation of the Popular Revolutionary Bloc (BPR), El Salvador's largest mass organization.

+ Tactics used by the government to discourage the opposition included even more blatant forms of intimidation. Alicia de Canizales, for example, candidate for mayor of Sonsonate, withdrew from the race after a paramilitary group called FALANGE threatened to kill all

her children.[89]

FAPU's founders. "There was a need for an organization representing popular sectors to present its own platform of demands."[90] FAPU comprised peasant and teachers unions, as well as representatives of the university; many of its original members subsequently left to form other organizations. El Salvador's largest mass organization, the Popular Revolutionary Bloc, was formed in 1975.

The mid-1970s marked a new phase in Salvadoran politics, one in which coalitions of peasants, workers, students, and intellectuals pressed their demands outside the traditional party system. In place of reformism and democratic openings, the popular organizations spoke of building socialism. Mass-based political activities dormant since 1932 began again.

The Molina government had limited resources with which to buy off growing unrest. The prices of El Salvador's commodity exports and processed goods could not keep pace with rapidly rising oil prices and the soaring cost of manufactured goods. Rural unemployment in 1973 reached 57 percent;[91] industrial growth slowed as investment was reduced to a trickle. In 1975 and 1976, Molina attempted to implement a limited agrarian reform program, which would have benefited about 12,000 peasants by redistributing approximately 1.4 million acres of land.[92] Only one peasant union, the government-favored Salvadoran Communal Union (UCS), supported the measure. The modest effort was blocked, however, by the powerful landowners' Eastern Region Farmers' Front (FARO), which saw "creeping communism" in the assault on the principle of private property. Later, El Salvador's Archbishop Oscar Romero would tell the oligarchy, "Open your hands! Give up your rings! Or the day will come when they cut off your hands."[93] In the late 1970s, the intransigence of the right as economic conditions deteriorated accelerated the process of disenfranchisement.

The Fraud of 1977

"The frequency with which elections are conducted in El Salvador . . .
insures that virtually no prolonged difficulties of any sort can escape
aggravation by the demands of electoral politics."
— Stephen Webre
José Napoleón Duarte and the Christian
Democratic Party in Salvadoran Politics, 1979.[94]

When the political opposition decided to participate in
the 1977 elections, it did so not because the elections
represented an opportunity to acquire power, but because
no other alternative was viable. Despite the repeated
trammeling of democratic aspirations, most centrist
politicians in 1977 still were not ready to endorse the
popular organizations—much less the guerrillas—as a
political alternative for El Salvador. Thus, in a lackluster
attempt to spark interest in a "return to democracy," the
UNO coalition formed in 1972 presented the ticket of retired
Army Colonel Ernesto Claramount for president, and
former Mayor of San Salvador José Antonio Morales Ehrlich
for vice-president. The official party, the PCN, nominated
Defense Minister Carlos Humberto Romero.

The extent of the fraud in 1977 shocked even the most
cynical. On election day, military radio transmissions
intercepted by UNO officials instructed local PCN officials
to stuff the ballot boxes—put more "sugar" (votes for the
PCN) than "coffee" (votes for UNO) in the "tank" (ballot box).
Military and paramilitary groups assaulted or intimidated
voters at the polls and evicted UNO inspectors from voting
areas. In most places, UNO officials were prohibited from
supervising the vote count. In the 16 municipalities where
an honest tally was taken, UNO won by a margin of 3 to 1.[95]
Nevertheless, five days after the election, the Central
Elections Council declared General Romero the winner.

The capital exploded into angry protest. Colonel
Claramount led a group of 50,000 to 70,000 citizens to the
downtown *Plaza Libertad,* where peaceful demonstrations
continued for several days. Workers in several factories and
transportation unions declared a general strike. The Army
and National Guard detained more than 200 UNO officials.

On February 28, heavily armed members of the security
forces ordered protestors to abandon the central plaza. As
some began to leave, the police opened fire. When the

shooting died down, nearly 100 lay dead in the main square.*[96] Claramount and Morales Ehrlich took refuge in a neighboring church, and were offered asylum in Costa Rica. "This is not the end," proclaimed Claramount as he was whisked toward the airport in a Red Cross ambulance. "It is only the beginning."[97]

In the spring of 1977 the struggle inside El Salvador began to be influenced by events abroad. President Jimmy Carter had taken office proclaiming his commitment to human rights: El Salvador, with its low strategic importance to the United States+ and record of serious human rights abuses began to attract attention. President Carter declined to send a presidential envoy to the inauguration of General Romero, and left the post of ambassador empty for several months.

Moreover, in its first annual budget presentation to Congress, the Carter administration reduced military aid to the Salvadoran Army. In retaliation, El Salvador joined Guatemala, Argentina, and Brazil in rejecting U.S. assistance outright. In El Salvador's case, however, the gesture was largely symbolic. Aid had been suspended by President Gerald Ford, after Salvadoran Army Chief of Staff Manuel Alfonso Rodríguez was convicted in New York of trying to sell several thousand machine guns to the U.S. mafia.[99]

While Washington dealt in symbols and the State Department spoke of "distancing" itself from the regime, conditions inside El Salvador worsened after the 1977 elections. In his first months in office, General Romero voiced appeals for national unity and reconciliation; but the land-owning elite and sectors of the military, bolstered by their victory over Colonel Molina's attempt at agrarian reform in 1975, called for the blood of the popular organizations. Strikes, work stoppages and land seizures organized or supported by the BPR, FAPU and LP-28 escalated dramatically throughout 1977. In

---

* The popular organization Popular Leagues-28th of February (LP-28) took its name from the day of the massacre.

+ In 1977, Deputy Assistant Secretary of State for Inter-American Affairs Charles W. Bray III stated that " ... the United States has no strategic interest in El Salvador; we do have an interest in the general tranquility and progress of the region."[98]

response, the army unleashed a new wave of repression, targeting the Church, labor, and especially peasants. "These violations of rights of ... opponents of the government," said the International Commission of Jurists in 1978, " ... are not isolated incidents due to an excess of zeal on the part of members of the security forces, but form part of a deliberate campaign to preserve the privileged position of the ruling minority."[100]

One of the more notable victims of the Army's crackdown was Father Rutilio Grande, a Salvadoran Jesuit, killed by machine-gun fire on his way to say mass in town outside Aguilares. Grande had been an outspoken defender of peasant union rights, and one month before his death had accompanied a group of parishioners protesting the expulsion from El Salvador of a Colombian priest. "Beware you hyprocrites with clenched teeth," he had warned local landowners, "who call yourselves Catholics and are full of evil ... You have no right to say 'I have bought El Salvador with my money, because this is a denial of God ....'"[101] The National Association of Private Enterprise and another landowner organization, the Eastern Region Farmers' Front (FARO) accused Grande and other priests of fomenting revolution and inciting class warfare. Grande's death marked the beginning of a vicious campaign against the clergy.

Additional reprisals followed his assassination. In May, FPL guerrillas kidnapped and executed Salvadoran Foreign Minister Mauricio Borgonovo, a member of the oligarchy. The right-wing vigilante White Warrior's Union (UGB), which announced its formation during Borgonovo's captivity, responded by killing another priest, Alfonso Navarro. Then, in June, the UGB issued a threat to all Jesuits to leave the country within a month or be executed. A flyer that circulated at the time urged Salvadorans to "Be a patriot! Kill a priest!"[*][102]

---

* One of the effects of the campaign against the Church was to radicalize its highest Salvadoran official, Oscar Arnulfo Romero, who had taken over as archbishop in 1977 with a reputation for conservatism. The abuses also focused an international spotlight on Salvadoran authorities, and Church officials in other countries began to speak out about conditions in El Salvador.

In November 1977, the Romero government abandoned talk of national unity in favor of a more vigorous campaign to establish "law and order." A legislature controlled by the official party passed a harsh Law for the Defense and Guarantee of Public Order, giving the government broad powers to arrest and try "subversives," break up public meetings, and ban strikes. The law was an attempt to provide a legal premise for official repression. But it ultimately hurt the regime, so intensifying international criticism that important foreign loans and credits from international lending institutions were suspended.

While the law was in effect, the left staged at least 40 labor strikes in defiance.[103] Ineffective and counter-productive, the law was repealed in February 1979.*

By early 1979, El Salvador's economy was declining rapidly. The private sector responded to labor unrest by shutting down factories and sending capital abroad. Industrial growth fell to a low of 3 percent in 1978; between 1978 and 1979, El Salvador's exports fell 10.5 pecent.[105] The ranks of the urban unemployed swelled, and conditions in the countryside—exacerbated by chronic low prices for coffee in the international market—deteriorated. Per capita income, already low even by Latin American standards, fell 1.6 percent annually betwen 1974-78.[106] The explanation for these economic problems was found in political instabiliy and unrest; worsening economic conditions, in turn, fueled popular protest.

By May 1979, when General Romero called for a National Forum to address the deepening political and economic crisis, Salvadoran society was irreparably divided. Landowners continued to call for harsh repression of the popular movement, but urban industrialists and some government and military officials, concerned by the reduction in foreign credits and the

---

* In the first six months the law was in effect, government troops violently broke up six strikes and two peaceful land occupations, attacked participants in at least eight demonstrations, and captured and tortured four priests. The Salvadoran archdiocese listed 790 victims of the law by June 1978, including 716 captured, 29 killed, and 45 wounded. Amnesty International recorded more than 200 cases of "disappearances" between 1976 and August 1978.[104]

international reputation of the regime, began to discuss the possibility of an *apertura política*.

The activities of the popular organizations, meanwhile, reached unprecedented levels: groups staged sit-ins at embassies, churches, the Red Cross, and United Nations offices to protest government repression and press their demands for socio-economic changes. In the middle of the year, labor strikes and factory occupations became more numerous. In March, electrical workers cut off power to the entire country for 23 hours, forcing a resolution of other labor conflicts. In May, events came to a climax when the National Police opened fire on peaceful demonstrators occupying the Metropolitan Cathedral to protest the arrest of five leaders of the BPR. At least 23 were killed and 37 wounded in full view of reporters and television crews.[107] The structure of Salvadoran society had broken down almost entirely.

In preparation for the National Forum called by the government, Romero lifted a state of seige and tried to enlist the help of the National Assembly Chairman Leandro Echeverría to bring about a dialogue with the country's moderate opposition. The Christian Democrats, the Church, and the popular organizations rejected the appeal, insisting that first the government had to proclaim a general amnesty, disband the death squads, and end government repression. As a result, the National Forum in August 1979, turned into a monologue, with only the official party and the private sector participating.

In response to the government-sponsored "dialogue," sectors of the opposition organized a "Popular Forum" *(Foro Popular)* to discuss alternatives to the current government. Participating in the *Foro* were four opposition parties, including the Christian Democrats and Social Democrats, as well as eight labor and peasant unions, and one of the popular organizations.* The *Foro* issued a platform calling for the return of political freedoms, short-and long-term economic measures to

---

* In retrospect, the *Foro Popular* appears to be the precursor of the middle-class alliance with the popular movement represented by the Revolutionary Democratic Front (FDR).

improve the lives of the majority rural population, and "effective participation of the popular organizations to guarantee a process of real democratization."[108] The Common Platform of the *Foro* became a blueprint for the program of future governments.

In the spring of 1979, U.S. officials in Washington became aware of the extent of the Salvadoran crisis. The State Department, vexed by the failure of its efforts throughout the winter of 1979 to mediate a solution to the Nicaraguan civil war, paid increased attention to events in the rest of Central America, especially El Salvador, where violence was escalating at an alarming rate.

In August and September 1979, Assistant Secretary of State for Inter-American Affairs Viron Vaky and special emissary William Bowdler* made secret trips to the Salvadoran capital. In keeping with the cautious human rights policy of the Carter administration, the two U.S. offficials urged General Romero to institute token reforms—move up elections and release political prisoners—to ease domestic tensions.[109] (Some reports held that they asked Romero to step down.) However, the Pentagon and National Security Council were urging a reinstatement of military aid to El Salvador to help the Army combat unrest.[110] Thus, inside the Carter administration, El Salvador was already shaping up as a crucial test of the human rights policy. Inducements to improve human rights could be voiced as long as the fundamental stability of the regime was ensured. Because that was no longer the case in El Salvador, it appeared that human rights might have to take second place to restoring internal order.

In mid-September 1979, a moderate Salvadoran business figure surmised that only a coup could break the stalemate between General Romero and the increasingly broad-based opposition. "There is a lot of unrest in the Army," he stated, "but there are some officers who favor a hardline solution and others who feel that it is time for the

---

* Bowdler had been the head of the U.S. team participating in the mediation effort in Nicaragua. In January 1980 Bowdler succeeded Vaky as Assistant Secretary of State.

army to step out of politics." Then he pinpointed the struggle that would consume the energies of the Salvadoran government for the next year and a half. "It is a question," he said, " of which group seizes power first."[111]

THE FIRST JUNTA

In the early morning hours of October 15, 1979, the sixty or so junior officers who had planned Romero's overthrow declared a coup d'etat and the formation of a new government. They had already elected two representatives—Colonel Adolfo Arnoldo Majano and Colonel Jaime Abdul Gutiérrez—to a new junta, and on October 12 had approached Román Mayorga, rector of the Catholic University, to join as one of the civilian members. Mayorga accepted on the condition that the *Foro Popular* be allowed to elect another of the civilians to serve on the junta. The military indicated that it would find a third candidate, and allow civilians a plurality in the new directorate.

"Military insurrection," declared Román Mayorga on the day of the coup, "is justified by repression and corruption, and the socio-economic structure of the country which is the main reason for its misery and poverty."[112] The armed forces accused the Romero government of "creating economic and social disaster" and "countenancing corruption, discrediting the country and the institution of the military."[113]

The junior officers created a new political body—the Permanent Council of the Armed Forces (*Consejo Permanente de la Fuerza Armada*—COPEFA)—within the military to represent their views and ensure that the evolving government remained true to the principles of the coup. In the Proclamation of the Armed Forces they proposed:

- to put an end to violence and corruption;
- to guarantee the observance of human rights;
- to adopt measures to bring about an equitable distribution of the national wealth, while at the same time rapidly increasing the gross national product; and
- to channel the country's foreign relations in a positive direction.[114]

Mayorga turned to the *Foro Popular* to elect its representative to the junta; after debating whether or not to participate in the new government, the *Foro* chose Guillermo Ungo, secretary general of the National Revolutionary Movement (MNR). Colonel Gutiérrez then approached the Salvadoran private sector to name a third civilian. The Chamber of Commerce agreed on Mario Andino, manager of San Salvador's Phelps Dodge affiliate and a friend of Gutiérrez since his days at ANTEL.* Now complete, the junta began to implement its platform, passing decrees over the next several weeks that disbanded the paramilitary group ORDEN, reduced the price of food staples, set a minimum wage for agricultural workers, nationalized the coffee export sector, and established a commission to investigate the fate of political prisoners and the *"desaparecidos."*

In the eyes of its makers, the coup appeared to be a chance—perhaps the last—to head off a revolution in El Salvador by, in the words of Mayorga, "initiating a process of profound reforms without bloodshed."[116] Indeed, the Proclamation of the Armed Forces embodied proposals to change the distribution of land ownership and wealth in El Salvador, structural reforms that challenged the economic hold of the oligarchy and offered substantial benefits to the majority of Salvadorans. The reformist announcements of the junior officers, moreover, appeared to signal that the armed forces as an institution were ready to abandon their role as guarantors of the status quo and to assume a new one that promoted change that would lead to a more equitable social and economic order.

However, to say that the coup also took place to guarantee the integrity of the armed forces as an institution was to state a basic contradiction. For while they agreed about the necessity of change, military officials were deeply divided over the scope and pace of proposed reforms, as well as over the methods for handling the popular movement.

Almost immediately after the coup, a series of maneuvers began that promised to thwart the reform

---

42 * Phelps Dodge was the sole provider of copper cable to ANTEL.[115]

process.[117] Key military officers, skeptical or hostile to the reforms and more concerned with repressing the left, began to assume strategic positions. On the day of the coup, Colonel Gutiérrez appointed his former boss at the National Telecommunications Company (ANTEL), Colonel José Guillermo García, to the post of defense minister. García, a candidate for the PCN's presidential nomination in 1976, had served a kind of exile as commander in the volatile province of San Vicente, where he earned a reputation for using harsh methods against militant peasant organizations. As the director of ANTEL in October 1979, García occupied a strategic post for military intelligence.

Without consulting civilians in the junta, García and Gutiérrez then appointed Carlos Eugenio Vides Casanova as director of the National Guard, and Carlos Reynaldo López Nuila as head of the National Police. Both belonged to a core of hard-line Army officers. García named his former subordinate at ANTEL, Colonel Nicolás Carranza vice-minister of defense. The High Command—a new "*oligarcia*"—had none of the fresh look of the junta or its reformist officers.

The orientation of the High Command, and its disregard for the authority of the junta, became apparent within days of the coup. Civilians on the junta ordered troops not to fire on unarmed demonstrators, and forbade soldiers to use force to dislodge workers who occupied five factories at the time of the coup. But on October 16, government troops burst onto the shop floors to break a strike, killing 18 workers and arresting 78 others.[118] In the first week of the new government, at least 160 people died in confrontations with police. "The security forces are repressing in a brutal manner," declared Archbishop Romero in mid-October, "more brutal that the former regime, because they are trying to prevent the new government from gaining credibility."[119]

While opposition parties—the PDC, MNR, and UDN—welcomed the coup and agreed to participate in the junta's newly formed cabinet, the left felt the coup was a betrayal of their cause. Popular organizations and the guerrillas denounced the change as simply "Romerism without Romero," and increased their activities. One group, the LP-28, called for all-out insurrection; later they radically changed their position and were among the first of the popular organizations to call for a provisional truce with the government. Within ten days of the coup, the BPR was holding approximately 300 hostages in the Labor, Planning, and Economic Ministries, demanding lower food prices, higher wages, and the release of still unaccounted-for political prisoners.*[120] The popular organizations wanted changes and wanted them immediately. With the exception of FAPU, the groups rejected dialogue with the junta, maintaining that as long as the armed forces were intact, the promises of changes were empty.

By failing to appreciate divisions within the military and between the civilian and military representatives of the junta, the left played into the hands of the coup's betrayors. The High Command and sectors of the Army and security forces furthest to the right ordered a stepped-up campaign of violence and repression on the premise of restoring "law and order." The junior officers acquiesced to their superiors, who warned that in a state of war, the most important principle was unity within the ranks of the armed forces.[122] The attitude of the left caused the younger officers to feel that they, too, were regarded as the enemy.

The High Command also enacted measures to break the power of COPEFA within the armed forces; COPEFA, with elected representatives from each *cuartel* or barracks, substituted internal democracy within the armed forces for the hierarchy based on rank. By December, García was claiming that "as for COPEFA, we have succeeded in converting it to a body of administrative consultation."[123] On several occasions, high-ranking military officers planned their own acts of sabotage against the military, blaming them on the left. In one incident, National Guardsmen entered the San Carlos barracks in the capital and killed three soldiers, leaving

---

* A government commission set up to investigate the fate of those arrested or missing under the previous regime had found no trace of more than 200 persons believed jailed or who had disappeared. Instead of political prisoners, investigators discovered clandestine jails and places of torture.[121]

behind leftist banners and propaganda designed to illustrate "who the real enemy was." When officers with knowledge of the incident gathered to protest, García threatened them and urged them to keep silent, saying that military men "could start killing each other for this" if the news leaked out.[124]

Officials of the United States embassy, which initially endorsed the coup, did little to encourage the announced reforms. U.S. Ambassador Robert Devine met with civilian members of the junta only twice while the first junta was in power, on visits that principally were to comply with protocol. Devine did, however, have more contact with the military representatives on the junta, as did the military attache at the embassy.[125] Both emphasized above all the need to restore law and order. In November, the United States sent its first—and only—aid to the first junta. It was a shipment of riot control equipment along with technical advisers to "professionalize" the operations of the security forces working to control the left.[126]

On December 7, as the death tolls from increased confrontations between civilians and the military mounted, the Cabinet told the junta of its concerns regarding the new government. Cabinet members said reforms were not being carried out, and that the junta was being used by "anti-popular and reactionary interests"[127] which continued to repress the civilian population. Ungo admitted that within several weeks of taking office, he had realized that power lay with the High Command, not the junta or the junior officers. "The principal problem we face, " he said, "is that the Army still views as the principal enemy not the oligarchy, but the organizations of the left."[128]

The day after Christmas, Cabinet members requested a meeting with the junta to discuss their concerns. Military officers learned of the request, and showed up uninvited. National Guard chief Vides Casanova spoke on behalf of the High Command. The junta was too tolerant of the popular organizations, he said, and civilians in the government were creating difficulties by discussing the problems of the lack of reforms and the continuation of repression. The Army did not need the civilians, he 45 claimed in a rude tone, to do what had to be done. Vides in essence was inviting the civilians to leave the government.

Then, Vides turned to García and stated that he was their *hombre de confianza,* and that the Army recognized his authority above that of the junta's. Vice-Minister of Defense Carranza echoed the endorsement. The message to the civilians was clear: the Army would continue with its repressive measures, and did not recognize the junta's authority. Even the civilians who had tried to keep an open mind regarding the role of the Army recognized after the December 26 meeting that they had no choice but to resign—or remain as window-dressing for a government controlled by the military.[129]

They next day, on December 27, 1979, Ungo, Mayorga, members of the Cabinet and several officers from COPEFA gathered in the Ministry of Agriculture. The only possibility remaining, they concluded, was to call on COPEFA to reassert its authority—and loyalty to the junta—as well as to meet certain conditions: carry out the reforms, end the repression. The civilians drew up an ultimatum. They gave COPEFA two days to respond.

On January 1 and 2, Archbishop Oscar Romero made an effort to mediate the crisis. The Church—as well as the civilians—feared that a collapse of the junta would inexorably lead to a worsening of the repression and ultimately to civil war. As the group met in the offices of the archdiocese, national radio stations broadcast COPEFA's reply. The statement, in essence, was a capitulation to the High Command.

"COPEFA is not a political body," the junior officers said, "but rather one founded to maintain the unity of the armed forces. The vehicle of communication between the junta and the High Command is the Ministry of Defense."[130] Several Cabinet ministers resigned immediately (one, Education Minister Salvador Samayoa, then announced his entry into the FPL guerrillas). The next day, January 3, Ungo and Mayorga and all but one of the Cabinet ministers—Colonel García—resigned in protest.

U.S. State Department officials accused civilians in the junta of being quitters, of failing to persist in their efforts. 46 "How can you expect in three months to change everything you've been talking about for 20 years?" they asked.[131] Internal divisions and inefficiency could have been overcome, U.S. officials claimed. But those who submitted their "irrevocable resignations" on January 3 had a different analysis. "The false notion of the neutrality of the military as an institution ... has generated a rightward turn in the process of democratization and social change," Ungo and Mayorga charged. "Under these conditions, the Revolutionary Governing Junta has only minimal, and essentially formal power."[132] Cabinet ministers were equally uncompromising. They denounced the "inclusion in the present government of reactionary forces who are tied in their very roots to the oligarchy" and criticized the "failure to achieve closer ties with popular movements who existence and importance can no longer be ignored."[133]

THE GOVERNMENT
MOVES RIGHT

Only one party, the Christian Democrats, appeared willing to renew the pact with the military. As early as the Cabinet crisis of December 27, the PDC, led by José Napoleón Duarte, who had just returned from exile, began to negotiate with military officers. After the mass resignations, the Christian Democrats approached members of the National Revolutionary Movement (MNR) to join them in a new coalition. U.S. Ambassador Devine, and a special emissary from the U.S. Embassy in Mexico, Jon Glassman, also encouraged members of the MNR to participate in forming a new junta.[134] The Social Democrats refused.

When Christian Democrats Hector Dada and José Antonio Morales Ehrlich became part of the second junta in mid-January, conditions were less than promising for putting together a new government. It took the party almost six weeks to fill all the Cabinet positions; some officials headed two and even three ministries simultaneously.

Meanwhile the opposition began to coalesce. Three popular organizations, along with the National Democratic Union (UDN), formed the Revolutionary Coordinating Council of the Masses (*Coordinadora Revolucionaria de Masas—CRM*) to unify and lead the popularly-based opposition. They called for a mass demonstration—the March of Unity—on January 22, the day commemorating the ill-fated uprising of 1932. At least eighty thousand persons filled the streets, carrying the banners of the BPR, FAPU, LP-28 and UDN. But as the marchers rounded the corner of one of the capital's major thoroughfares, they were attacked by sharpshooters stationed on the rooftop of the National Palace. The crowd dispersed in panic, leaving more than 20 bodies strewn on the streets.[135] Archbishop Romero condemned the killings from his pulpit at the Metropolitan Cathedral. The military High Command stiffened.

By February, hard-line officers inside and outside the

goverment had begun to tire of civilian juntas and talk of reform. Rumors of a coup, to be headed by Colonel Nicolás Carranza and retired General José Alberto Medrano spread through the capital. The U.S. Embassy, which had kept a low profile, went into action. Military attache Jerry Walker and Washington's special emissary, acting chargé d'affaires James Cheek argued with the High Command.[136] They told the military leaders that a coup by the right would only enhance the long-term prospects of the left because the legitimacy of the government—which was being maintained by civilian representation in the junta—would be eliminated by a takeover. Promised military and economic aid would not be delivered, they threatened. As evidence of U.S. support for the Army, Cheek proposed the sending of 36 U.S. military advisers to train Salvadoran troops in the logistics of professional counterinsurgency. Dada was sickened by the idea of what Cheek had called a "clean counterinsurgency war."[137]

Right-wing officers did not stage a coup, but the would-be instigators retained their posts. However, the effects of the threat of a coup began to reverberate through the ranks of the Christian Democratic party. Morales Ehrlich sent an ultimatum to the military, saying that if those responsible for the coup were not removed in seven days, the Christian Democrats would withdraw from the government.[138] On March 3, the deadline, only Dada followed through with the threat. "We have not been able to stop the repression," he stated as he resigned from the junta, "and those committing acts of repression disrespective of the authority of the junta go unpunished ... the chances for producing reforms with the support of the people are receding beyond reach."[139]

Duarte replaced Dada on the junta, culminating a decades-old bid for national power. But the Salvadoran political center had begun to wither away. The Christian Democrats—who would face subsequent defections from their own ranks—stood alone in alliance with the military.

The Carter Policy

Following Dada's resignation, Washington's involvement in Salvadoran politics increased dramatically. A new ambassador, Robert White, arrived in early March 1980. He was known as a liberal in the wake of his defense of human rights in Paraguay, ruled by General Alfredo Stroessner.* White's arrival coincided with a clarification of U.S. goals in El Salvador. If the left was to be contained, reforms would have to be pressed forward immediately. If the government was to gain any credibility, violence and atrocities by security forces would have to be controlled. "Washington wants something to the right of Nicaragua," White declared in private as he prepared to leave for the Salvadoran capital. "My job is to make that happen."

Within days of White's arrival, the Salvadoran government initiated the long-promised agrarian and banking reforms.+ On paper, the reforms were among the most sweeping in Latin American history. The first phase was to involve seizure of all properties of more than 500 hectares (1250 acres); the former owners were to be paid in cash and government bonds. These properties were to be turned over to peasant cooperatives. The second phase, planned for a later date, was to involve seizure of *haciendas* of between 150 and 500 hectares (375-1250 acres). These *haciendas* comprised the heart of El Salvador's coffee lands. Another phase, not announced at the time but subsequently drafted by the AFL-CIO's affiliate, the American Institute for Free Labor Development (AIFLD), was described by its title, "land-to-the-tiller." It was designed to make sharecroppers the owners of their tiny rented plots. The agrarian reform thus had two central and complementary objectives: to break the oligarchy, whose resistance to change was seen

---

* White's nomination as ambassador was held up in the Senate for several weeks by Sen. Jesse Helms of North Carolina, who opposed White as being too liberal.

+ Of all the reforms announced at the time of the October coup, only one—the nationalization of the coffee and sugar export sectors—had been carried out.

as fueling the forces of revolution, and to weaken the left by removing a source of popular grievance and creating a large group of peasants loyal to the government.

U.S. proposals for reforming the Salvadoran military contained a similar counterrevolutionary logic. Having learned from the experience of Nicaragua, U.S. officials in the State Department and Embassy argued that excessive violence by goverment troops only brutalized the population, guaranteeing a steady stream of recruits for the guerrillas. The message emanating from Colonel Eldon Cummings, the U.S. military commander in the Embassy in El Salvador was unequivocal. "We are telling the High Command that they are defaming the very institution they are trying to preserve," he explained in mid-1980.[140]

The United States began to provide the funds and equipment for "clean counterinsurgency." On March 3, 1980, the State Department forwarded to Congress a request for $5.7 million in "non-lethal" military aid for El Salvador, including equipment such as trucks, jeeps, communications gear, and night vision devices to improve the Army's maneuverability and infrastructure. Officials told Congress the equipment "would help strengthen the Army's key role in reforms" and provide the necessary leverage for the United States to pressure the government to reduce the killing. They added that the aid would help strengthen the hand of progressive civilians and reform-minded officers in the government, who were trying to control violence from the "extremes of the right and the left."[141] Images of the Salvadoran junta and military carefully nourished in Washington began to take hold.*

Between the time the aid request was introduced, however, and the time it was approved, some of the neat characterizations of Salvadoran politics presented by U.S.

---

* That the Salvadoran conflict was perceived within a regional context was evident by other aid requests made at the time of the $5.7 million proposal for El Salvador. The Pentagon, arguing in favor of $3.5 million in arms credits as well as the lease of 10 helicopers to Honduras, stated that "the Hondurans believe, and our intelligence concurs, that Honduran territory is being used to channel arms and insurgents from Cuba to El Salvador." Congress approved the aid to Honduras, along with the aid to El Salvador.[142]

officials began to fray at the edges. The number of Salvadorans who considered themselves to be in the political center declined rapidly following the March 1980 announcement of the agrarian reform plan, a measure designed to expand rather than erode the government's base. Government ministers and Christian Democratic Party officials, who left the ruling coalition in droves, harshly condemned the increase in repression that paralleled the implementation of the agrarian reform measure.[143] To some of these Salvadoran officials, agrarian reform was no more than another aspect of the government's counterinsurgency campaign—carried out by the military under state of seige provisions to further their efforts to undermine leftist *campesino* unions.* Other officials noted that the passage of the reform occurred simultaneously with a steep increase in repression throughout the country, which undercut peasant's confidence in the reform and impeded its implementation.[145]

The Christian Democrats themselves were bitterly divided by the controversy. On March 10, during the party's convention, the PDC's Popular Faction, with 20 percent of the convention's delegates, withdrew from the party, stating that the PDC "should not participate in a regime which has unleashed the bloodiest repression ever experienced by the Salvadoran people."[146] The same day, seven members of the Christian Democratic leadership, including former junta member Hector Dada and party founder Roberto Lara Velado, resigned from the party. "A program of reform with repression runs contrary to the fundamentals of Christian Democracy," they charged. "The program of structural reforms ... loses all effectiveness if not implemented in a climate of freedom; which is to say, unless accompanied by the

---

* This interpretation of the agrarian reform is reflected in a press release by Amnesty International on March 17, 1980, calling on the Salvadoran government to "halt a campaign of murder and abduction against peasants.... Hundreds of men, women and children are believed to have been killed and many more forced to flee their homes.... Troops operating in open coordination with the paramilitary organization ORDEN have shot or abducted peasants, razed villages, and destroyed crops ... "[144]

cessation of all repression and the democratic participation by the organizations representative of the people."[147]

In the weeks that followed, the party officials were joined by eight Cabinet ministers and undersecretaries charged with administering various aspects of agrarian reform.*

A congressional Appropriations subcommitee began meeting on March 25, 1980, to consider the request for $5.7 million in military aid to El Salvador. Their deliberations began in an atmosphere charged by a far more spectacular event—the assassination on March 24 of San Salvador's Archbishop Romero, who had been gunned down while saying mass in a hospital chapel. The previous Sunday, he had given a sermon in which he called on "the troops of the National Guard, the police, and the garrisons"[149] to disobey orders to kill that violated the law of God.

Church officials close to Archbishop Romero said his assassination was the work of the Salvadoran right. The Archbishop had earned their emnity by championing the rights of the poor and for his strong condemnation of government repression of popular organizations.† In the view of the right, however, Romero seriously overstepped his bounds when he used his moral authority to call on Salvadoran soldiers, particularly young draftees with a religious upbringing, to disobey their superiors. The Salvadoran spiritual leader's statements had begun to

---

* Many of the officials who subsequently resigned, particularly Finance Minister Roberto Alvergue Vides and Planning Minister Roberto Salazar Candell, took issue with several technical aspects of the reform. The most controversial was Decree 207—land-to-the-tiller— drafted in close cooperation with U.S. advisers from the AFL-CIO's American Institution for Free Labor Development (AIFLD) without consultation with Salvadoran officials.[148]

---

† Shortly before his death, Archbishop Romero stated that " . . . Christians do not fear combat; they know how to fight, but they prefer to speak the language of peace. However, when a dictatorship seriously attacks human rights and the common good of the nation, when all becomes unbearable, and the channels of dialogue, of understanding, of rationality are closed; when this occurs, the Church speaks of the legitimate right of insurrectional violence."[150].

threaten the foundations of the armed forces.*

Although they made statements deploring Romero's death, U.S. Congressmen who met on March 26 to vote on military aid to El Salvador interpreted it within the framework provided by the State Department, which presented the assassination as an example of the type of extremist violence that the Salvadoran government needed to control. Members of the House subcommittee were not insensitive to the charges of repression and violence committed by government security forces, but believed that the best answer was to lend support to junior officers of the Army in the hopes that their "progressive vision" would prevail. Legislators expressed the belief that if they did not support the existing coalition, extremists on the left or right would take power, and the country would move closer to an all-out civil war.

The subcommittee voted 5-3 on April 1 to approve the aid. One Democratic congressman described the vote as "the most agonizing one I've had to make in years."[152] It was not the last time that Congress would reluctantly go along with administration proposals because they could perceive no satisfactory alternatives.

The Opposition Coalesces: Formation of the FDR

If Romero's death deprived El Salvador of one of its voices for unity and conciliation, it also gave impetus to the opposition groups to attempt to bury their differences and establish broad coalitions. On April 2, 1980, still distressed and angry from the ordeal of the previous week, a group of ex-government ministers, independent

---

* Documents captured with retired National Guard Major Roberto D'Aubuisson in May 1980 included a personal diary that, in the opinion of Ambassador Robert White and Salvadoran experts, outlined the plan for the Romero assassination. *"Operación Piña"* called for "one sharpshooter, four security men, one Starlight telescopic sight and one driver." It also included the names of right-wing Salvadorans, many of whom lived in exile in Miami, who White and others believed
54 financed the assassination.[151]

professionals, nonaligned unions, the Social Democrats and dissident Christian Democrats met at the Catholic University to announce the formation of the Salvadoran Democratic Front (FDS).* The 14 groups associated with the FDS saw their organization as analogous to the Broad Opposition Front (FAO) that had formed in Nicaragua to unite the opponents of the Somoza regime. "We are giving the Salvadoran people the benefit of our experience," said FDS President Enrique Alvarez Cordoba in a press conference, "in order to form a broad front in support for their stuggle."[153] Implicit in Alvarez's statement was the recognition that the "democratic experiment" represented by the first civilian-military junta formed in October 1979 was a failure, and that only closer collaboration with the left could bring about significant social and political changes in El Salvador.

U.S. Embassy officials attended the FDS press conference. So did leaders of the executive council of the popular organizations, the CRM, which had already begun a dialogue with representatives of the FDS concerning unification of their two movements. Two weeks after the formation of the FDS, the efforts at consolidation bore fruit.

The Salvadoran Revolutionary Democrat Front (FDR) was founded on April 18, 1980. It merged the 12 groups of the Democratic Front with the four popular organizations that comprised the CRM.+ The Front elected Enrique Alvarez, former agriculture minister and representative of

---

* Groups in the Democratic Front included the National Revolutionary Movement (MNR), Popular Social Christian Movement (MPSC), National University of El Salvador (UES), Association of University Students (AGEUS), Independent Movement of Professionals and Technicians (MIPTES), Salvadoran Association of Bus Companies (AEAS), Federation of Salvadoran Workers (FENASTRAS), Federation of Food, Clothing, and Textile Workers (FESTIAVTCES), Revolutionary Federation of Unions (FSR), United Federation of Unions of El Salvador (FUSS), Union of Social Security Workers (STISS), and Union of Workers of United Industries (STIUSA). Observors included the Catholic University "José Simeón Cañas" (UCA), and National Federation of Small Business (FENAPES).

+ The Movement for Popular Liberation (MLP) joined the CRM in the spring of 1980.

the Movement of Independent Technicians and Professionals (MIPTES) as its president, and adopted as a working platform the proposal drawn up by the CRM for a "revolutionary democratic government."*

The Front recognized the armed groups of the left as its "vanguard"—those who would lead the struggle. On April 24, 1980, Alvarez said, "only a government that results from the triumph of the people's struggle, as the CRM has suggested and which the FDR accepts and supports, can make possible a new society."[155] The leaders of the democratic opposition—former government officials, professionals, members of centrist parties—had traveled a long road. The failure of their own efforts to achieve reform through existing structures and a series of juntas was leading them to endorse armed struggle and seek as political allies the groups comprising El Salvador's mass movement.+

Following the formation of the Front, political initiative in El Salvador shifted to two opposing blocs: a center-left coalition including armed groups as well as professionals and former officials of the first and second juntas; and rightist sectors of the military in alliance with increasingly ineffectual Christian Democrats. The two blocs were not without their own internal tensions, but the State

---

* The platform of the Revolutionary Democratic Front established as some of its first tasks the "overthrow of the reactionary military dictatorship of the oligarchy and Yankee imperialism, imposed and sustained against the will of the Salvadoran people for fifty years ... and to put an end to the overall political, economic, and social power of the great lords of land and capital ... "[154]

+ The FDR differed in an important way from the Broad Opposition Front in Nicaragua, to which it has often been compared. In Nicaragua, th dissident intellectuals, clergy, and members of the private sector who formed the Front joined in the fight against Somoza to defend their own interests. In El Salvador, members of the former "democratic opposition" who joined the Front did so to endorse the program of the revolutionary opposition—that is, they joined without a separate agenda. In July 1980, Guillermo Ungo said, " ... in Nicaragua ... the alliances of classes in opposition to Somoza included the weakened national bourgeoisie. Right after the Sandinista victory, the bourgeoisie moved to recover its influence and had to be edged out, slowly and painfully. In El Salvador, the class alliance has been distilled ... There can be few surprises we won't be prepared for now."[156]

Department's contention that Salvadoran politics were characterized by a centrist coalition besieged by extremes of the left and right was largely a myth. The center had ceased to exist, except on paper.

The D'Aubuisson Affair

In May 1980, another coup attempt against the government illustrated both the inability of the Christian Democrats to exercise effective power, and the growing marginalization of the leader of the moderate wing of the Army, Colonel Majano. On May 7, Majano ordered the arrest of a group of right-wing activists suspected of plotting a coup from a farm outside San Salvador. The raid produced ex-National Guard Major and intelligence chief Roberto D'Aubuisson, along with several military officers, documents relating to the proposed coup, and personal papers. The subsequent "D'Aubuisson Affair" (there have been several, including D'Aubuisson's entry and public appearances in the United States after having been declared *persona non grata* by Ambassador White) had all the elements of tragicomedy.

The day after the arrests, outraged Christian Democrats threatened to withdraw from the government if D'Aubuisson and his cohorts were not "tried and sentenced." San Salvador's Mayor Julio Adolfo Rey Prendes declared that "the Christian Democracy is not disposed to continue in this process if higher pressures compel the release of those implicated in the coup d'etat."[157]

Three days later, however, "higher pressures" intervened. A military judge, after consultation with Colonel García, claimed that there was "insufficient evidence" to prosecute D'Aubuisson. On May 13, one week after the arrest, García himself went to the prison where D'Aubuisson was held to release him.[158]

The Christian Democrats reneged on their ultimatum and remained in the government. The officer corps of the Army, meanwhile, voted in secret ballot to replace Majano as head of the armed forces with Colonel Gutiérrez, "to put an end to the dual situation in the leadership of the military institution."[159]

The D'Aubuisson affair confirmed what many critics of the Carter administration's policy in El Salvador had charged: that the military was less interested in controlling instances of rightist violence than it was in cracking down on the left, and that power in the military had shifted away from the reformers of the October coup and their civilian counterparts.

The rightward swing in the military corresponded to an increase in the level of guerrilla activity. Battles took place throughout the spring and summer in the northern provinces of Chalatenango and Morazán, and around the Guazapa volcano in the province of San Salvador. The guerrillas used traditional methods of unconventional warfare, including hit-and-run attacks designed to wear down the Army's morale and ability to respond. As the threat of more generalized conflict increased, the military closed ranks behind its rightist leadership, which subordinated efforts at reform to military campaigns to eliminate guerrilla insurgency. The kind of "clean counterinsurgency" advocated by the Carter administration gave way to full-scale terror in the countryside. Reports in the U.S. press of human rights violations committed by the Salvadoran armed forces began to include those of massacres against the civilian population.*

By deciding on a policy of counteroffensive in the rural areas and repression of the political opposition in the cities, the Salvadoran Army helped shape the balance of power on the left in favor of armed groups. Following government reprisals against the March of Unity on January 22, 1980, the leadership of the CRM decided to de-emphasize demonstrations and mass rallies that exposed participants to the Army. Work stoppages in March and June, nevertheless, met with success. But a general strike called by the FDR in August 1980 was a failure, in part because of strong countermeasures undertaken by the government and the left's inability to protect the strikers.

---

* One such event occured in May 1980, when Salvadoran troops killed nearly six hundred persons attempting to flee fighting in the northern provinces. Soldiers fired on peasants attempting to cross the Sumpul River into Honduras; Honduran soldiers formed a cordon on the opposite bank of the Sumpul and prohibited the refugees from entering Honduran territory.[160]

Police threatened bus owners and drivers with reprisals if they did not maintain normal service, and tens of thousands of government employees were told they would lose their jobs if they joined the strike. Soldiers in battle dress patrolled the streets of the capital before and during the strike; approximately 60 percent of factory workers appeared at their jobs rather than risk dismissal.*[161]

The intensification of the war effort, moreover, exacerbated differences among the armed groups of the left. Debate intensified within the guerrilla ranks—nominally joined in May 1980 under the Unified Revolutionary Directorate (DRU)—concerning the proper strategy and tactics for fighting the regime. "Prolonged popular war" factions stressed the need for a long-term strategy of continous assaults against the military and political work among the peasantry. "Insurrectionists" argued that a military defeat of the Army was impossible, and that the left should seek a rapprochement with petty bourgeois sectors of the population as well as with progressive military factions. In August, the debate became public when the Armed Forces of National Resistance (FARN) withdrew from the DRU.+

---

* To protest the government arrests and firings that occured during the August strike, 1,500 employees of the Rio Lempa hydroelectric company blacked out the country for 20 hours. The military responded by taking over the national electric, water supply, and telecommunications networks under the provisions of a state of emergency declared on August 23.

+ Remaining groups accused the FARN of being "adventuristic, coup-inclined, individualistic, and hegemonistic"[162] for pressing an insurrectional strategy that involved close contact with the "democratic and honest sectors of the armed forces." The FARN maintained, however, that its proposals for even greater integration of the revolutionary groups into a Single Party of the Salvadoran Proletariat (PUPS) were being resisted by the leadership of "sister organizations."[163] The FARN reentered the DRU in mid-November, several weeks after the formation of the Farabundo Martí National Liberation Front (FMLN), which comprised all guerrilla forces. The debate over strategy included disagreements concerning what constituted the correct decision-making process within the guerrilla directorate. The FARN argued that since each of the groups within the DRU maintained its own structure and identity, the leadership should reach decisions by consensus. The FPL, ERP, and PCS argued for majority rule.

In the early Fall of 1980, the crisis within the left ran parallel to another crisis within the military. The kind of full-scale counterinsurgency campaign envisioned by the High Command could not coexist with Majano's orientation toward dialogue with the left, and his continued opposition to the repressive tactics used by sectors of the Army and security forces. On September 1, 1980, Colonels García, Carranza, and Gutiérrez, without consulting Majano, issued the monthly "order of battle," a schedule of assignments and rotations. All Majano's supporters were stripped of their command posts and shifted to desk jobs or to embassies in foreign countries. For several days the capital was rife with rumors of an impending coup, a violent division within the ranks of the Army, or the beginning of a full-scale insurrection. Ultimately, however the *Majanistas* acceded to the order, in exchange for a weak assurance that the civilians in the junta would be consulted regarding future assignments.

The September orders marked a stunning defeat for Majano and his followers, many of whom had become too concerned with the institutional preservation of the Army in the face of increasing threats from the left to challenge their superiors.

Dialogue: Attempt and Failure

On September 23, the Episcopal Conference of the Salvadoran Catholic Church made an effort to slow the country's descent into civil war. The six bishops issued an "anguished and pressing" call for a national dialogue to stop the "violence ... death, hatred, and vengeance" that had claimed 6,000 lives since the beginning of the year.[164] Even before the proposal was formally presented to the Salvadoran government, Christian Democrats and Colonel Majano responded favorably; but elements within the military, if they believed in the concept of dialogue at all, began to set their own preconditions for talks—which included a demand that the left lay down its arms. Before the Salvadoran government officials could reach an agreement among themselves, the left responded. "We cannot sit down to talks," stated FDR

President Alvarez, "with a government that is not part of the solution but part of the problem."[165]

Leaders of the popular organizations went further, arguing that because of the conservative nature of the Catholic hierarchy, the Church did not have the "moral authority" to mediate. The failure of the Church's effort in the fall of 1980 thus reflected not only divisions within the Salvadoran government, between civilians and hard-liners within the military, but also the left's lack of confidence that dialogue would mean anything more than betrayal.

The overt position of the U.S. Embassy was to support the Church's attempt at mediation, but U.S. officials had already embarked on a parallel course designed to divide and weaken the left. Assistant Secretary of State for Inter-American Affairs William Bowdler attempted during a July trip to the Salvadoran capital to convince affiliates of the FDR to split with their Marxist-Leninist allies and support the Christian Democrats in the government. The best hope for peace, Bowdler argued, was in "expanding the center," and the real interests of the "democrats" within the FDR coalition, he maintained, lay not with the revolutionary left but with other civilian reformers.[166] The same message was delivered to an FDR delegation, which included Enrique Alvarez, that visited Washington in late summer.[167] The FDR responded negatively to U.S. proposals that tried to reconstitute the center-left coalition of the first civilian-military junta in October 1979. "The State Department contradicts its own words," explained FDR leader Rubén Zamora. "On the one hand they tell us that we are so weak that some alleged madmen on the left will eat us alive. On the other hand, they urge us to go in with the junta so that it can rely on our strength to break the oligarchy."[168]

In late November, six FDR leaders were abducted from a meeting in a Jesuit high school in San Salvador and later murdered. Although Defense Minister García denied any government involvement in the killings, Church officials claimed that about 200 uniformed soldiers had surrounded the high school while heavily armed men in civilian dress kidnapped the six leaders.[169] Their mutilated bodies appeared on the outskirts of San Salvador the following day.

61

The death of the six leaders had profound consequences in El Salvador and abroad. The left, convinced of the government's complicity in the murders, said that the proposal for a dialogue while the armed forces remained intact appeared to have been thoroughly discredited. Duarte, Morales Ehrlich, and Majano faced a stark choice in the wake of the killings: accede to the right's *de facto* takeover of the government, or resign and go into exile.

For the United States the challenge was no less complete: the killings made a mockery of U.S. attempts to pressure the military to improve human rights, promote reforms, and support a political reconciliation with the left. Rather than retracting their earlier characterization of the Salvadoran government, however, Carter administration officials looked for new ways to resurrect its image. They believed that withdrawing support would lead to the outcome the administration feared most—a triumph of the left through armed insurrection.

THE U.S. CONTEXT OF SALVADORAN AFFAIRS

Part of the sharp swing in Salvadoran politics in late 1980 resulted not only from increased guerrilla activities but also from political developments in the United States. The election of Ronald Reagan on November 4 emboldened the Salvadoran right. President-elect Ronald Reagan—in a campaign speech to the Chicago Council on Foreign Relations that presaged the way in which he would frame his policy toward El Salvador—had affirmed that "in El Salvador, Marxist totalitarian revolutionaries, supported by Havana and Moscow, are preventing the construction of a democratic government ... Must we," he asked, "let ... Grenada, Nicaragua, El Salvador, all become additional 'Cubas,' new outposts for Soviet combat brigades? ... These humiliations and symbols of weakness add up."[170]

The two themes of Reagan's policy—that revolution in El Salvador was a question of external manipulation and that "taking a stand" in El Salvador was necessary to reverse perceptions of U.S. global impotence—became the backdrop in San Salvador for assessments by the Salvadoran right of what they could get away with until January 15.*

For the Salvadoran private sector, Reagan's electoral triumph appeared to presage a general foreign policy shift to the right, and at least a lack of vigorous support for the reforms in El Salvador. A delegation of private sector representatives who visited Washington in late November was told that the United States would increase economic and military aid, but that the Reagan administration would not tolerate a military coup that ousted the Christian Democrats, and would not seek a reversal of the agrarian and banking reforms.[171] Like Carter administration officials, members of Reagan's transition team

---

* The day Reagan won, rightist assassins attempted to blow up Colonel Majano's vehicle as his motorcade passed in front of the Salvadoran Agrarian Reform Institute (ISTA).

recognized the need for civilian participation in the Salvadoran junta in order to maintain the appearance of the government's legitimacy. The agrarian reform was also considered necessary to maintain the junta's reformist image, although implementation of additional phases would not be pressed by Reagan administration officials. What the private sector representatives heard, in essence, was a modified version of the Carter administration's message: the private sector would receive additional support for their efforts to influence political events and rebuild El Salvador's economy, but could not turn back the clock to the era before October 1979.

The Salvadoran military, however, interpreted the Reagan victory as a license to kill. The top U.S. priority, they reasoned, was defeating the armed groups of the left. To do that, the United States needed the Salvadoran Army, and other policy objectives would be subordinated to the end of waging effective warfare. Ultimately, however, it was the Carter administration that would vindicate the Army's assessment, but not before the Salvadoran junta, and Carter officials, faced one last test of the role of Carter's human rights policy in dealing with El Salvador.*

The Murder of the Churchwomen

On December 2, Ursuline Sister Dorothy Kazel and lay missionary Jean Donovan went to El Salvador's international airport in their white Toyota minibus to meet arriving Maryknoll Sisters Ita Ford and Maura

---

* The period of the "inter-regnum" from November 4, 1980 to January 20, 1981, was marked by a bitter dispute between Reagan transition team officials Pedro San Juan and Frank Carbaugh and U.S. Ambassador Robert White. The Reagan Latin Americanists leaked to the press a report saying that " ... Ambassadors are not supposed to function in the capacity of social reformers and advocates of new theories of social change with latitude to experiment within the country to which they are accredited."[172] White retorted that such statements were undercutting his authority and that of the Christian Democrats and were inviting the right wing to take a bolder stance.

Clarke. Ford and Clarke had taken a later flight to El Salvador than planned, coming from Managua, Nicaragua where they had been attending a Maryknoll regional meeting. None of the four women was aware that others in the airport were also awaiting their arrival. "No, she didn't arrive on that flight," said a member of the Salvadoran security forces over a pay phone in the airport when the 4:45 p.m. flight from Managua landed. "We'll have to wait for the next."*

Ford and Clarke arrived about 7 p.m. At approximately 10:30 that evening, peasants near the village of Santiago Nonualco saw the sisters' white bus pass their houses. Then they heard a short burst of machine-gun fire, followed by three or four single shots.[174]

The burnt-out Toyota van was found beside the airport road the next day. On December 4, the bodies of the four churchwomen were exhumed from a deep common grave about an hour's drive from the airport. Autopsies revealed that two had been sexually abused before they had been killed.

The murder of the four U.S. churchwomen brought U.S. policy into sharp relief. Ambassador White, an acquaintance of the four missionaries, vowed that "they [the killers] won't get away with this." On December 5, one day after the bodies of the four women were exhumed, the State Department "put a hold on all economic and military assistance commitments," stating that "reports of involvement of the security forces [of El Salvador] are a matter of deepest concern."[175]

Carter dispatched to San Salvador a team that included Assistant Secretary of State for Inter-American Affairs William Bowdler and Kissinger's former Under Secretary of State William Rogers to investigate "reports of involvement of the security forces" in the murders. The investigating team actually had a dual mission, because in the wake of the murders, the Salvadoran political situation became increasingly chaotic. Rogers hinted that

---

* Maryknoll Sister Marie Rieckleman was on the 4:45 p.m. flight, but instead of staying in El Salvador she was continuing on to Miami. During the layover in San Salvador, three Salvadoran soldiers boarded the plane and through the stewardess, questioned passengers about their destinations. The stewardess returned twice to Rieckleman. "Are you sure you're going on to Miami?" she asked. "Are you sure?"[173]

the team would do more than investigate the killings when he stated before leaving Washington that the group would attempt to find "what kind of government can exercise power effectively in El Salvador's conditions."[176]

As Rogers spoke, Christian Democrats were negotiating with the military for greater control of the government. The day after the team's arrival in El Salvador, Colonel Majano—who had continued talks with the left throughout the fall—was forced to leave the governing junta following a no-confidence vote by the Army. Several days later, Colonel Gutiérrez said, "I was ordered to cut out the cancer of infiltration even within the government junta itself."[177] The State Department, which had once called Colonel Majano "80 percent of our policy," did not protest.

A reshuffling of the Salvadoran government was announced several days after the Bowdler mission left El Salvador.* Duarte was belatedly appointed president of the junta, the post denied him in 1972 by some of the very officers now governing at his side. Colonel Gutiérrez became vice-president and Commander in Chief of the armed forces, ending formally any illusion of civilian control of the military.+ El Salvador finally had a civilian president, albeit unelected, a move that would facilitate U.S. support of the government. "I am the last bullet," declared Duarte following the reshuffling, a statement more indicative of the desperate nature of the regime than of any claim to legitimacy.[178]

---

* From San Salvador, members of the U.S. team flew to Tegucigalpa, where they attended the signing of the peace treaty between El Salvador and Honduras, which restored diplomatic and commercial relations that had been broken after the 1969 war. The treaty left some border issues unresolved, but ended the status of a six-kilometer wide demilitarized zone between the two countries, making it accessible to the armies of each side in their respective territory.

+ Other changes in the High Command were announced, to take effect in January 1981. They did little to alter the balance of military power—rightists such as Vice-Minister of Defense Colonel Carranza were removed from posts in command of troops, while others, such as Colonel Rafael Flores Lima, secretary of information during the Romero regime, were brought back into senior positions.

The State Department moved quickly to endorse the changes by restoring economic aid on December 17; it called the restructuring of the government "positive developments" and cited the Salvadoran government's "commitment to a thorough, professional, and expeditious investigation of the killings" of the four churchwomen.[179]

The Bowdler-Rogers report had concluded that the Salvadoran High Command was not involved in the murders, but that lower-level members of the security forces might have been.* Its conclusion was broad enough to deflect any charges of U.S. complicity in a cover-up, but also ensured that the subsequent investigation—or lack thereof—would not interfere with the overall goal of U.S. policy—providing support for the Duarte government.+

---

* On March 18, 1981, Secretary of State Alexander Haig suggested to the Senate Foreign Relations Committee that the nuns were killed "in an effort to run a roadblock," a theory dismissed by State Department officials—including then-Deputy Assistant Secretary of State James Cheek—closely involved in the investigation. In May 1981, Salvadoran authorities arrested six low-level members of the security forces for their alleged involvement in the murders. The six were arraigned on February 10, 1982 and one was released. Family members of the slain churchwomen claim that the investigation stopped short of identifying who had given the orders to kill the women. In November 1981, former Salvadoran Vice-Minister of Planning Carlos Federico Paredes described a Cabinet meeting in the Presidential House two weeks before the women were killed in which Defense Minister García stated that nuns and priests in the north of El Salvador were "influencing the people to struggle against the government" and that "we've got to take steps against the missionaries." García brought in during the meeting a 10 year old boy from Chalatenango, where Ford and Clarke were living, who said that nuns and priests in the area were collaborating with leftists.[180]

+ The assassination of Rodolfo Viera, a peasant union leader and head of the Salvadoran Agrarian Reform Institute (ISTA), along with two American specialists from the AFL-CIO's American Institute for Free Labor Development (AIFLD) on January 3, 1981, further compromised the State Department's support for the Salvadoran government. Colonel Majano, who had gone into hiding following his ouster from the junta, accused the Salvadoran military of knowing who was responsible for the killings. Shortly before his death, Viera had begun to publicize instances of military corruption and fraud within ISTA that involved as much as $40 million.[181]

The Guerrilla Offensive

The crisis-ridden month of December culminated with reports that the long-promised guerrilla offensive in El Salvador was about to begin. FMLN guerrilla commander Fermán Cienfuegos told reporters in Mexico that the rebels would present the incoming Reagan administration with an "irreversible situation" on the day of Reagan's inauguration: guerrilla units throughout the country had received orders to take up combat positions, and the start of fighting was to be accompanied by a crippling general strike.[182] The call to insurrection came on January 10, scarcely ten days before Carter was to leave office.*

The immediate response of the Carter administration contained the seeds of Reagan's subsequent policy. Military aid was increased, advisers were dispatched, accusations of foreign involvement by communist powers were made, and sanctions against Nicaragua were adopted. While the Carter measures in retrospect were mild compared with the subsequent Reagan initiatives, the actors and themes of Carter's group set the stage for an increased U.S. commitment to the Salvadoran government.

First came the renewal of military aid, which had been suspended after the deaths of the four U.S. churchwomen. The State Department announced on January 14 that "the leftist guerrillas ... demonstrated that they are better armed and constitute a military threat" and "received a substantial supply of arms from abroad."[183] Indeed during the early fighting, there had been a mutiny in Santa Ana, one of the most important garrisons in the country, and numerous officers had defected to the guerrilla ranks. But charges of foreign involvement in an arms flow to the rebels were more difficult to substantiate. A Salvadoran Cabinet minister said, "nothing has

---

* At the start of the offensive, the newly established Political-Diplomatic Commission of the FDR-FMLN announced in Mexico that it was willing to seek a political solution to the conflict to minimize the certainty of massive bloodshed. The Political-Diplomatic Commission, with seven members from groups comprising the FDR and FMLN, carried out the international diplomatic work of the Front.

changed here ... weapons have been coming from Cuba, Russia, China, and Nicaragua for over a year. The only change has been in your country."[184] President Duarte and Colonel Gutiérrez said at the time that the guerrillas' main source of arms was the black market, and that their most powerful weapons were still those made in the United States.[185]

Nonetheless, Ambassador White affirmed that the "quantity and sophistication" of weapons sent from outside "weighed heavily" in the U.S. decision to resume military aid. Then, in a statement that he later retracted, White claimed that "approximately 100 men" had landed on January 14 at El Salvador's El Cuco beach from Nicaragua, and that the evidence was "compelling and convincing."*[186] The administration suspended disbursement of outstanding portions of a $75 million aid package to Nicaragua, and quickly authorized an additional $5 million in emergency military aid to the Salvadoran Army. This time the tone was harsher. "We must support the Salvadoran government," said the State Department on January 17, "in its struggle against left-wing terrorism supported covertly with arms, ammunition, training, and political and military advice by Cuba and other Communist nations."[188] By the time President Carter left office, twenty U.S. military instructors were in El Salvador, training Salvadoran officers in various aspects of counterinsurgency techniques and planning, and lethal weapons—machine guns, grenade launchers, ammunition, and helicopters—were being provided by the United States for the first time in nearly four years.

The guerrillas thus made two fundamental errors in starting the fighting—overestimating their own strength and failing to understand that a lame duck president in

---

* In startling testimony before the Senate Foreign Relations Committee in April 1981, White stated that he had become "skeptical of the reality of that invasion" in which "no one was captured and no battle took place." (White's evidence in January of the foreign invasion was that the men had ostensibly arrived in boats made of wood not native to El Salvador.) White also questioned the nature of military intelligence, which, he stated, was "intended to serve a particular kind of solution." At another point in his testimony, White said, "The record of military intelligence in Central America is abysmally bad."[187]

the United States did not mean there was a power vacuum in this country. U.S. resolve not to "lose" El Salvador was a concept deeply rooted within the permanent bureaucracy that prevailed on national security issues, no matter who was president.

The Reagan Response

While these shifts in policy on the eve of the departure of the Carter administration laid the groundwork for escalation under Reagan, they were not carried out within the framework that the new administration would place around Third World issues. "We consider what is happening [in El Salvador] is part of the global Communist campaign coordinated by Havana and Moscow to support the Marxist insurgency," said Secretary of State Haig to a group of NATO ministers in mid-February.[189]

The message was clear: El Salvador was no longer just a local conflict in the United States' traditional sphere of influence, but a direct result of Soviet meddling—"risk-taking" in Haig's words. The tone adopted by the administration indicated that regional policy would be cast in the spotlight of East-West conflict. Several weeks after his statement to the NATO ministers, Haig charged that the Soviet Union had a "hit list" in Central America, and that the first objective had been the "seizure of Nicaragua."[190]

El Salvador, in retrospect, must have appeared to U.S. officials as an appealing place to "draw the line" against communism and reassert U.S. global power. The guerrillas' "final offensive" of January had failed to set off a nationwide insurrection, leading U.S. policymakers to conclude that the rebels lacked popular support. State Department and Pentagon officials believed that it might be possible to defeat the rebels simply by cutting off major supply lines and providing sufficient military aid. By acting tough and drumming up publicity for its anti-communist stance, the administration could then claim victory for its new, assertive policy. However, this simple formula was based on several erroneous judgments. First, the administration underestimated the level of public, congressional, and allied opposition to a policy of Cold War belligerence. Second, Reagan officials miscalculated guerrilla strength. The January offensive, while falling short of its ultimate objectives, did advance and consolidate rebel positions in key parts of the country.*

To prepare the press, Congress, and the public for an escalation of U.S. military aid and advisory support, the administration in early February began to leak portions of documents allegedly captured from the guerrillas detailing Soviet, Cuban, and Eastern bloc support for the insurgents. Haig told a group of NATO ministers on February 17 that "a well-orchestrated international Communist campaign designed to transform the Salvadoran crisis from the internal conflict to an increasingly internationalized confrontation is under-way."[192] He asserted that most of the Soviet-bloc weapons had entered El Salvador through Nicaragua. The administration terminated $9.6 million in food aid to Nicaragua on February 10, pending a review of Nicaragua's involvement in funneling arms to El Salvador. Simultaneously, Deputy Secretary of State William Clark told Latin American diplomats that the United States intended "to go to the source with whatever means may become reasonably necessary" to stop the alleged arms flow from Cuba.[193]

The threats were followed by a diplomatic offensive. Haig dispatched high administration officials—Lawrence Eagleburger, Lieutenant General Vernon Walters, and Luigi Einaudi—to the capitals of Europe and Latin America to seek Allied support for U.S. policy. They carried with them an inch-thick "White Paper" on "Communist Influence in El Salvador" prepared by the

---

* As military hostilities died down, President Duarte stated that " ... this is not the end ... We cannot call this a victory. The revolutionaries have their machinery established. Their leaders are trained. They have support from abroad. They have thousands of active supporters."[191]

State Department to prove the charges of Eastern bloc interference.*

The "truth squads" that traveled through Europe and Latin America encountered at best a mixed reception to the White Paper. Few leaders challenged the authenticity of the captured documents, and several even applauded the tough anti-Soviet stand, but even staunch Allies expressed reservations about the excessive concern with military remedies for the Salvadoran crisis. Such diverse governments as those in Mexico, Argentina, Venezuela, and Brazil, went on record opposing deeper U.S. military involvement in El Salvador, even though they held widely divergent opinions regarding the Salvadoran left and the legitimacy of its claim to power.†

But the greatest challenge to the Reagan offensive came from within the United States. Members of the U.S. Congress and public saw the dispatch of military advisers to El Salvador as a "Vietnam scenario" of spiralling commitments and involvement. Senator John Glenn and 45 members of the House charged that sending U.S. personnel might be a violation of the War Powers Act,

---

* Even before the rhetorical dust had settled, Reagan administration officials outlined the steps they would take to stop the 'Communist onslaught" in El Salvador. These included dispatching 20 additional "non-combat advisers," including Green Berets, to train Salvadoran army troops, sending an additional $25 million in military aid to El Salvador, and leasing additional helicopters to the government.[194] Notably absent from the official communiques was any mention of the issues that had ostensibly shaped U.S. policy in the past—the promotion of reforms, and an improvement in the observance of human rights. Instead, the administration underscored the military aspects of a solution to the Salvadoran conflict, an emphasis that cost it dearly when it tried to marshall support for the policy.

---

† West Germany became the first major U.S. ally to set itself apart from the U.S initiative, with sources close to Chancellor Helmut Schmidt saying that the solution to El Salvador's problems must be political, not military. Foreign Minister Jean Francois-Poncet of the French government of Valéry Giscard d'Estaing released a statement saying that although there was public concern with "external interference" in El Salvador, the problem could not be solved "by purely military means." Following meetings between President Reagan and Canadian Prime Minister Pierre Trudeau in early March, the Canadian Minister for External Affairs, Mark MacGuigan, publicly opposed the U.S. decision to send arms and advisers to El Salvador.[195]

which requires congressional notification when U.S. forces are sent to participate in "hostilities" or might have an "imminent involvement in hostilities." Gallup polls taken in March showed that less than 2 percent of the U.S. public favored U.S. military intervention in El Salvador and that 80 pecent were skeptical of the wisdom of sending advisers.[196] The U.S. Catholic Church, as well as other religious and human rights groups, continued to raise questions about the nature of the Salvadoran government and especially the role of the Salvadoran military in political affairs. The Archbishop of Washington, Joseph Hickey, called U.S. policy "risky to the point of being reckless."[*][197]

The State Department responded to the criticism with a clumsy attempt to backtrack. In mid-March, Deputy Assistant Secretary of State for Inter-American Affairs John Bushnell told reporters that they were running the Salvadoran story "five times as big as it is,"[198] thus passing onto the press the responsibility for the administration's public relations failure. Bushnell later invoked a crude kind of McCarthyism when he made an accusation that protests of U.S. policy were the work of a "well-orchestrated effort" by a "world-wide Communist network."[199]

Another technique the administration used to counter domestic criticism was to claim success. The State Department claimed that the release of the White Paper and the initiative built around it had apparently slowed the infiltration of Soviet-bloc weapons into El Salvador. Almost a month later, officials asserted that the flow of arms through Nicaragua to El Salvador had "virtually stopped."[200] Whether this was based on reliable intelligence or was a product of the administration's need to claim victory is uncertain. What is clear, however, is that the question of an arms flow repeatedly was used as a rationale for new policy initiatives, regardless of whether any conclusive information existed to support them.

---

* Progress in the investigation of the murder of the four U.S. churchwomen was a major concern of the Catholic Church and civic groups. On February 11, the State Department confirmed that finding and identifying the killers of the four U.S. churchwomen was no longer a condition for continued U.S. aid to El Salvador.

Exposés that questioned the veracity of the White Paper illustrated this point. According to one published in March in the *Los Angles Times*, the White Paper charged that Soviet-bloc countries promised 800 tons of arms to the Salvadoran guerrillas, and that 200 tons had been delivered. The documents included in the White Paper, however, indicated that only about 10 tons of weapons had ever crossed the border into El Salvador.[201] The *Wall Street Journal*, in early June, carried a story in which Jon Glassman, the State Department official principally responsible for the White Paper, described parts of it as "misleading" and "overembellished." He noted that statistics cited in the document were often "extrapolations."

"The only concrete instance of Soviet aid delivered to the Salvadoran rebels reported in the 19 documents was an airplane ticket from Moscow to Vietnam for one guerrilla," the *Journal* reported.[202]

The arms flow issue was also cause for friction within the administration. Secretary of State Haig told members of the House Foreign Affairs Committee in mid-May that "massive shipments" of weapons to El Salvador had resumed, and were being sent from Cuba through Nicaragua and Honduras. Other State Department and intelligence agency officials, however, said that Haig's charges were exaggerated, and were based on reports stating that the Salvadoran Army thought the guerrillas near the Guatemalan/Honduran borders had more weapons than before.[203]

The credibility gap that the administration had created by tying in its anti-Soviet offensive with its policy on El Salvador soon had unanticipated consequences. In late April and early May, the House Foreign Affairs Committee and the Senate Foreign Relations Committee passed a measure placing conditions on the following year's foreign aid bill. Military aid to El Salvador would be restricted unless the president certified that basic conditions were being met. These included a reduction in human rights violations, greater government control over the Salvadoran security forces, and movement toward discussions that would involve all major parties to the conflict. (These conditions became law when the foreign aid bill was signed by President Reagan in December

1981.)* The fact that these conditions survived in a Republican-controlled Senate was further evidence of the lack of support for the tone and direction of administration policy. In the wake of this congressional action, State Department pragmatists began working to redefine the emphasis of U.S. policy in a way that might regain public support for the administration's activist stance in El Salvador.

In a major speech before the World Affairs Council on July 16, Assistant Secretary of State for Inter-American Affairs Thomas Enders made no mention of El Salvador as a place of East-West confrontation, declaring rather that "just as the conflict was Salvadoran in its origins, so its ultimate resolution must be Salvadoran." The speech, notably, did not herald any new direction in actual policy, but reaffirmed the U.S. commitment to extend "economic and military assistance to counter the disaster visited upon El Salvador by enemies of democracy." The speech did, however, emphasize "the search for a political solution" in El Salvador through elections open to "all parties that renounce violence."[206] Thus the United States could use support for the electoral process as evidence that it was not relying solely on a military solution, yet could continue to maintain its commitment to exclude the guerrillas from this process unless they gave up their arms—a move tantamount to surrender.

The shift to a milder tone regarding the policy toward El Salvador did not mark the end of the administration's preoccupation with foreign Communist intervention; it simply indicated that this concern had been thrust into the background for a time.

Meanwhile, during the summer, the Duarte government was buffeted by the most serious challenge to its rule since the offensive of January 1981. Part came from

---

* On January 28, 1982, President Reagan certified to Congress that "the Salvadoran government is making a concerted and significant effort to comply with internationally recognized human rights," and that there had been a "declining level of violence over the past year and a decrease in alleged abuses by security forces."[204] These statements were challenged by figures released by the Salvadoran Catholic Church, which showed an increase in noncombatant deaths from 1980 to 1981, as well as by Amnesty International, which stated that "the pattern of abduction, torture and murder reported in the Amnesty International Report 1981 was unchanged."[205]

the guerrillas, who launched a second phase of the "general offensive" in mid-July. The rest came from the Salvadoran private sector, which intensified its efforts throughout the summer and fall to remove the Christian Democrats from power, or at least achieve private sector representation on the junta.

The immediate targets of businessmen—whose private sector organizations the Productive Alliance (AP) and the National Association of Private Enterprise (ANEP) represented the majority of private capital in the country—were the agrarian and banking reforms enacted in March 1980, and the ideology of "communitarianism"— the collaboration of labor and capital in production and ownership—embraced by the Christian Democrats. "We are faced with only two choices," said Manual Enrique Hinds, leader of the Productive Alliance, "communitarianism and communism. A steely dictatorship only comparable to Marxist tyranny lies behind communitarianism."[207] Businessmen blamed the reforms for the perilous decline in the Salvadoran economy: a 9.5 percent reduction in gross national product in 1981; capital flight of between $625 million and $2 billion for the two-year period beginning October 1979; and a loss of $468.8 million in coffee and cotton export revenues in 1981 as a result of political violence.[208] But their claims masked a deeper desire: to govern El Salvador once again through an alliance with the military, which would take care of the guerrilla threat while they restored "prosperity" and "development" to the country.

The political offensive against Duarte* conducted by

---

* Principal vehicles for the right-wing challenge to President Duarte and the Christian Democrats were the elections for a Constituent Assembly, scheduled for March 1982. Two leftist parties affiliated with the FDR—the MNR and the UDN—were legally permitted to register, although they declined to do so. The other right and center-right parties included: the National Conciliation Party (PCN), traditional party of the military; the National Republican Alliance (ARENA), led by former National Guard Major Roberto D'Aubuisson, organizer of several coup attempts against the government as well as numerous political assassinations; the Popular Orientation Party (POP), led by ex-General José Alberto Medrano, founder of ORDEN; the Democratic Action Party (AD) led by lawyer René Fortin Magaña and supported by the private sector; the Renovating Action Party (PAR) led by businessman Ernesto Oyarbide; the Salvadoran Popular Party (PPS) founded when the PAR split in 1964 and including in its membership former members of the PCN.

the private sector met little resistance from the U.S. Embassy. In his first address as Ambassador to El Salvador, Deane Hinton told the American Chambers of Commerce that the future of El Salvador was "in your hands," noting that " ... your organization symbolizes and reinforces the tight bonds of friendship and commerce which unite the peoples of El Salvador and the U.S."[209] Hinton on several occasions intervened to prevent attempts to remove Duarte and the Christian democrats from the junta. But he also made it clear to businessmen that since the United States regarded them as the group that would salvage the economy, they could expect the Reagan administration to be more receptive to their demands.*

The political initiative conducted by the private sector weekend the Christian Democrats. What pushed the government to the brink of collapse, however, was a series of military successes for the guerrillas in August 1981. For ten days in the middle of the month, the guerrillas

---

* In his speech to the American Chambers of Commerce, Hinton indicated that new reforms would not be undertaken until "existing reforms" were "consolidated". This was, in effect, a promise that the United States would not press for implementation of the second phase of the agrarian reform, which provided for a takeover and redistribution of El Salvador's coffee lands.

On December 10, 1981, a pro-reform peasant federation, the Salvadoran Communal Union (UCS), issued a report stating that the "failure of the agrarian reform process is an immediate and imminent danger." The report said that:

* "at least 90 officials" and a "large number of beneficiaries" of the reform "have died during 1981 at the hands of the ex-landlords and their allies, who are often members of the local security forces;

* more than 25,000 sharecroppers or tenants had been forcibly evicted from their farms, "in the majority of cases with the assistance of members of the military forces;"

* 15,000 families eligible for individual ownership had gotten provisional title to land, but none had received permanent ownership;

* of more than 300 peasant cooperatives formed on large estates, only two had received title to the land.[210]

The State Department stated on January 25, 1982, that despite "deficiencies" and "implementation problems" in the land reform process, it nonethless constituted a "remarkable success."[211]

captured and held the town of Perquín near the Honduran border, and simultaneously waged a campaign of sabotage against economic targets. At one point, almost the entire eastern third of the country was blacked-out by attacks on the electrical system, and the capital of San Salvador was without electricity for three days.

On August 28, the military and political offensives conducted by the opposition converged. France and Mexico, in a move that embarrassed and angered the United States, recognized the FMLN/FDR as a "representative political force, prepared to assume the obligations and to exercise the rights that derive therefrom."[212] The declaration, while amounting to a step less than granting the rebels belligerent status, nevertheless served as an important endorsement of their legitimacy as a political force, and recognition—still denied by the United States—that they would have to be part of the process leading to a solution to the Salvadoran crisis.

Some of the French-Mexican declaration's force was subsequently diminished by a counterresolution signed by nine Latin American nations on September 2. That document was originally conceived as a statement by the Andean Pact countries. When key Andean countries such as Peru and Ecuador refused to sign on, the declaration's sponsors, Colombia and Venezuela, turned for support to the dictatorships of the Southern Cone and Central America. The final statement, signed by the foreign ministers of Venezuela, Colombia, Argentina, Bolivia, Chile, Paraguay, Guatemala, Honduras, and the Dominican Republic, criticized the decision of France and Mexico "to intervene in the internal affairs of El Salvador," and at the same time asserted that "a political and democratic solution to [the] conflict should only be sought for by the Salvadorans themselves, without any sort of direct or indirect foreign intervention."[213]

The spotlight on diplomatic activity shifted to the battlefield in early September. Reports from the field indicated that the guerrillas were inflicting heavy losses on the Salvadoran Army and causing significant damage to the economy. (In late July, Hinton released figures 78 compiled by the Salvadoran High Command that estimated the Army had suffered 1,300 casualties in the first six months of 1981, before the July-August offensive had begun.) On September 30, the guerrillas' *Radio Venceremos* announced the joining of two military fronts in eastern El Salvador, and government offensives in Morazán, Chalatenango and around the Guazapa volcano failed to dislodge the guerrillas. On October 15, the second anniversary of the military coup, the guerrillas blew up the Puente de Oro spanning El Salvador's Rio Lempa, one of two bridges on major highways linking eastern and western El Salvador. The destruction of the bridge raised the possibility that access to the provinces of Usulutan, San Miguel, Morazán, and La Union might be cut off, facilitating the creation of a liberated zone in the eastern third of the country. The guerrillas— characterized by President Carter as "constituting a military threat" when they launched their January offensive—for the first time appeared capable of winning the war.

The response of the Reagan administration to the changing picture on the battlefield was pessimistic but measured: "I think we are now observing a stalemate," said the head of the U.S. Southern Command, Lieutenant General Wallace Nutting, "and in that kind of war, if you are not winning, you are losing."[214] The reports from the field did, however, prompt a reassessment within the administration, not over the goals of U.S. policy—which remained the uncompromised defeat of the left—but over the means to achieve that objective.

Widening the Crisis

The issue of the "stalemate" in El Salvador also became the vehicle for a renewed regional initiative to strike at other administration targets—Cuba and Nicaragua. As in the spring, the charges of an increased arms flow to the Salvadoran guerrillas served as the ostensible reason for renewed administration concern. This time, however, the heightened rhetoric sounded less like a warning than like a commitment to action. "Our aim is to make the risks ...

of Cuban subversion and terrorism in the hemisphere ...
seem to be more costly than the advantages," said
Alexander Haig on October 29.[215] Later, before the House
Foreign Affairs Committee, Haig refused to rule out U.S.
involvement in efforts to overthrow or destabilize the
Nicaraguan government.[216] For the first time since the
Cuban missile crisis, the Cuban government put the
island on full military alert. Nicaraguan Foreign Minister
Miguel D'Escoto complained of "verbal terrorism."

The policy of "calculated uncertainty"—that is,
intimidation through the threat of force—represented
more than an attempt to cut off the arms flow to
Salvadoran guerrillas. It became the extension of a
decades-old policy of unremitting hostility toward the
Cuban revolution, and the linking of that policy to a
campaign against the second armed revolution in the
hemisphere in twenty years—Nicaragua. The contours of
the policy toward Cuba were announced and relatively
visible: a tightening of the economic embargo, the
opening of "Radio Free Cuba" to broadcast U.S. programs
to the island, and a propaganda offensive to publicize the
dangers of Cuban activism in Latin America.* The outlines
of the policy toward Nicaragua were less clear in late 1981,
although the charges against the country were not.

Part of the administration offensive against Nicaragua
centered on domestic policies adopted by the Sandinista
leadership. These included periodic closings of the major
opposition newspaper *La Prensa*, which the Nicaraguan
government said had not complied with laws regulating
the media, and the jailing of four leading private sector
representatives who, the government claimed, had
violated economic emergency legislation.+ U.S. officials

---

* A second White Paper, entitled "Cuba's Renewed Support for
Violence in the Hemisphere," was leaked to the press in late November
and presented to Congress on December 14.[217]

+ Jailed along with the four representatives of the Superior Council of
Private Enterprise (COSEP) were several leaders of the Communist
Party union Labor Action and Unity Federation (CAUS). All those
arrested were charged with violating two laws—a government decree
passed on July 20, 1979 prohibiting the "publishing, verbally or in
writing, statements, proclamations, or manifestos that are threatening

also were concerned about the Sandinista's failure to schedule elections before 1985. On NBC televison's "Meet the Press" on November 22, Haig complained of Nicaragua's "drift toward totalitarianism." The same day, presidential adviser Edwin Meese warned that the "hour was late" in Nicaragua.

Accusations about the direction of the Sandinista revolution paled in comparison with the administration's principal grievance. Assistant Secretary of State Enders and other U.S. officials asserted that Nicaragua was becoming a "platform for intervention" in Central America, and that its leadership was engaging in a military buildup engineered by the Soviet Union and Cuba that made the country a serious threat to the rest of the region.[220] Charges of an arms flow to the rebels in El Salvador took on a new aspect as Nicaragua was painted as a territorial aggressor. Under Secretary of Defense Fred Ikle said on December 15, "Nicaragua is now regularly violating Honduran territory in supplying the Salvadoran guerrillas." Later Ikle referred to "cooperative mutual security" efforts and to U.S. obligations under the Rio Treaty, which provide for joint action against an aggressor nation in the case of an external attack.[221]

As harsh rhetoric became veiled threat, however, visible policy remained the same. Aid remained suspended, and U.S. officials maintained that the principal point of contention impeding a *modus vivendi* between the United States and Nicaragua was the Sandinistas' foreign policy, including alleged support for the Salvadoran guerrillas and an internal military buildup. In the face of negative Allied responses (especially from Mexico) to the threats of intervention in Nicaragua, Haig softened his tone somewhat in early December at the Organization of American States General Assembly meeting, where he

---

to the national security and integrity, public security, and the national economy," and an economic and social emergency law passed on September 2, 1981, prohibiting the dissemination of "false information for the purpose of altering salaries and prices of goods, textiles, merchandise, stocks, deeds, and similar things . . ."[218] On October 19, 1981, COSEP leaders published a statement in which they criticized the "crumbling of the national economy," the government's "unmistakable Marxist—Leninist ideological line," and the "preparation of a new genocide" in the country.[219]

said it was still "too early" to say whether Nicaragua was on its way to totalitarianism.[222]. Simultaneously, however, State Department officials began informing members of congressional intelligence committees that covert activities were under way in Nicaragua to destroy economic targets for the ostensible purpose of interrupting supply lines to the Salvadoran guerrillas and to increase internal strife.* The harsh statements thus served as a smoke screen for an activist and covert U.S. policy to destabilize the Nicaraguan government.

---

* On Januray 9, 1982, the Nicaraguan government revealed what it said was a "vast conspiracy" to blow up industrial plants, including Nicaragua's oil refinery and cement factory, and assassinate government leaders. The alleged conspiracy, for which 15 plotters were arrested, allegedly involved Argentine, Honduran, and Venezuelan officials in coordination with the CIA.[223]

Beginning in February 1982, major newspapers and television networks in the United States began revealing details of U.S. covert activities in Nicaragua. The reports were based on leaks from within the Reagan administration, and stated that President Reagan had approved a $19 million budget for the CIA to build and fund a paramilitary force of 500 Latin Americans to conduct sabotage against economic targets—bridges, power plants, etc.—inside Nicaragua. According to National Security Council records, the CIA proposed in November 1981 the "support and conduct of political and paramilitary operations against the Cuban presence and Cuban-Sandinista support structure in Nicaragua and elsewhere in Central America."[224]

The 500-man unit was to be supplemented by a 1000-man force to be trained by Argentina. In addition, the plan envisioned use of former members of elite U.S. military units (i.e., the Green Berets) for "highly sensitive intelligence collection and demolition work."[225]

Another covert operation approved by the President and reported to Congress involved funding groups and individuals inside Nicaragua in opposition to the Sandinista government.[226]

CONCLUSION

At the beginning of President Reagan's second year in office, the commitment to the Duarte government intensified. In certifying to Congress that human rights in El Salvador had improved during that previous year, Assistant Secretary of State Enders declared that "the decisive battle for Central America is under way in El Salvador."[227] In San Salvador, U.S. Ambassador Deane Hinton remarked with unusual candor that " . . . we've never been looking for a military victory. Now we may be forced to where there's no real choice."[228] The statement was quickly disavowed by Enders, but was reflected in actual policy. In the first weeks of 1982, the Reagan administration began training 1,600 Salvadoran soldiers on U.S. soil, and provided another $55 million in emergency military aid—including, for the first time, a sophisticated arsenal of counterinsurgency jets and forward air control planes—after a daring guerrilla raid on El Salvador's Ilopango air base. Eighteen aircraft were destroyed or damaged in the attack.[229]

Just as cries of "another Vietnam" accompanied the dispatch of military advisers to El Salvador in March 1981, skepticism and alarm on the part of Congress and the public accompanied the increased involvement in 1982. Members of the House and Senate sent investigative missions to Central America, questioned the size of the commitment in the face of domestic budget cuts, and demanded to know if the administration saw "the light at the end of the tunnel."[230] The specter of Vietnam that hovered over the debate acquired new urgency in the face of administration statements: Enders presented a stark choice between the Duarte government and one dominated by Communist insurgents. By defining the latter as totally unacceptable and rejecting a middle path —negotiation —as "giving the country away,"[231] Enders set up El Salvador as an all-or-nothing proposition. The United States could back the Duarte government whatever the cost or suffer a defeat for U.S. interests. The prospect for an end to the war seemed more remote than ever.

83

As this brief study has attempted to illustrate, the causes of revolution in El Salvador have deep historical roots. Revolutions, as Fidel Castro learned painfully in the 1960s, are not exportable. Rather, they develop as a confluence of economic and political factors—as political stuctures fail to respond to changing economic and social realities, and the state's mechanism for maintaining order becomes another cause of discontent.

In El Salvador, revolution resulted from nearly a century of oligarchic economic control—reinforced and facilitated by decades of direct rule by the military. Groups in power refused to share it with new groups and classes emerging in times of economic boom. They also refused to use their power to address the needs of the marginalized in times of economic hardship. The result was a process of mass alienation, exacerbated by flagrant violations of political rules and the most elementary notions of justice. The possibility of revolution increased in El Salvador as individuals and groups became convinced of the system's inability to provide for either development or equity—a conclusion reached as channels for dissent and peaceful reform were diverted or blocked off entirely.

The fundamental error of the Carter administration was its belief that it had intervened in this process in time to stop it—that it could organize a credible political "center" where none existed; that it could change the function of the Army from repression to reform, if not overnight, at least in a matter of months; that it could render an economic elite politically ineffective by attempting to redistribute some of its enormous wealth.

The assumptions of the Reagan administration are equally flawed and more grotesque—that Marxist puppets at the long end of a Soviet string are fighting but have no links to local history or to the local population, and that defeating them is a question of snipping supply lines and mustering the sufficient dose of military will. If the bloody results of the last two years of Salvadoran history are any indication, two successive U.S. administrations have failed miserably to understand or address the "Salvadoran problem."

At the time this study is being written, the war in El Salvador has claimed more than 30,000 lives and made refugees of more than 600,000 people—13 percent of the Salvadoran population.[232] Minor skirmishes between government troops and guerrillas have evolved into full-pitched battles involving thousands of soldiers, tons of heavy equipment, and month-long seiges against rebel positions. The guerrillas show little sign of being weakened, however, and despite U.S. support, the morale and fighting ability of government troops appears unchanged, and may be flagging.

In the midst of war, the United States and President Duarte called for elections for a Constituent Assembly in March 1982 as part of a political solution to resolve the crisis. The proposal received an important endorsement from the eleventh meeting of the OAS General Assembly in December 1981. However, using elections to try to resolve the conflict raised important questions, even at the time elections were proposed. Would they end the fighting, or contribute to a process that could lend credibility to the regime? Did the climate exist in which contenders for power could campaign freely? Was the electoral process itself so discredited by years of military fraud that any results would be irrevelant? The impact of the elections will not be determined until months afterward. Pre-election politics, however, left little room for optimism about the possibility that the Salvadoran crisis could be alleviated by the ballot, or that votes cast at the polls could substitute for a more radical approach to a peaceful settlement.*

---

* In announcing U.S. support for an electoral solution, Enders called for the participation of "all groups that renounce violence," [233] an invitation to the guerrillas to participate after they had laid down their arms. Predictably, the FMLN-FDR rejected the call, noting that it was a proposal for unilateral disarmament that did not call for a similar commitment from the Army. The Salvadoran left instead repeated its call for a "comprehensive process of political negotiations" between the government and the opposition, stressing that elections were only one part of a broader mediated solution.[234]

The State Department used the left's refusal to agree to its terms as justification for a new publicity campaign. High-level officials claimed that the guerrillas were unwilling to seek at the polls what they could not win on the battlefield. The officials said the guerrillas had refused to contribute to the peace process, and had declined to open a dialogue with President Duarte concerning the terms of the elections. The administration's charges, however, ignored a central issue: that no

In place of the March elections, the FMLN-FDR made it clear that it supported mediation. Specific proposals were transmitted by the Nicaraguan goverment to the United Nations in October 1981.[*][236] These called for talks without preconditions on two basic issues—the creation of a "new political, economic, and social order," and a restructuring of the Army to include rebel units as well as soliders serving the junta. In February 1982, Mexican President José López Portillo carried the negotiation initiative even further. He offered a three-point peace plan for the region, including a mediated settlement of the war in El Salvador, a non-aggression pact between the United States and Nicaragua and U.S.-Cuban talks to ease mutual hostilities.[238]

A Zimbabwe Option?

Since mid-1981, the reference point for a negotiated solution has become Zimbabwe, where a guerrilla war that spanned nearly two decades was ended through talks involving the most important actors—guerrilla factions, the white Rhodesian government, and the major outside supporters of both sides. The metaphor of a "Zimbabwe solution" appears relevant to El Salvador, not only as a model for conflict resolution, but also as an example of the obstacles to and preconditions for successful negotiation.

Direct U.S. participation in the search for a solution to

---

one, least of all the Salvadoran military, could guarantee the safety of opposition candidates if they did decide to participate in the campaign. If the murder of six leaders of the FDR in November 1980 did not provide sufficient proof, the Salvadoran Army provided additional evidence, in March 1981. Just as election plans were getting under way, the Army issued a "hit list" of 138 "subversives" and "traitors to the fatherland." The list included church officials, human rights activists, and virtually all opposition leaders that the State Department wanted to return from exile to El Savador to "campaign freely."[235]

---

[*]On January 27, 1982, the five top commanders of the FMLN sent a letter to President Reagan calling for a negotiated end to the war.[237]

the Zimbabwean conflict began in 1976. In the wake of the victory of the Popular Movement for the Liberation of Angola (MPLA) in Angola, Secretary of State Henry Kissinger sought ways to prevent the further radicalization of countries in southern Africa. Kissinger's efforts were based partly on the conviction that the longer the war in Rhodesia continued, the more radical its solution would be. In 1976, a victory by the Patriotic Front guerrillas was by no means assured; but rather than take any chances, the Ford administration decided to push for negotiations, which U.S. officials felt would produce a more moderate outcome than a rebel victory through force of arms. Negotiation, therefore, was a means of moderating the postwar government's policies, ensuring a place for whites in the future administration, and preserving the property rights of white farmers.

The Reagan administration has rejected Kissinger's view, and indeed embraced its opposite, refusing to negotiate in order to deny guerrillas at the bargaining table what U.S. officials believe they could not win on the battlefield. However, the same possibility exists in El Salvador that existed in Zimbabwe—the longer the war continues and the more the rebels gain by force of arms, the more radical the government that ultimately emerges will be.

The issues involved in the settlement of the Zimbabwean conflict and those in El Salvador seem to be similar: a restructuring of the armed forces and a redefinition of the socio-economic order. In Zimbabwe, the formation of new military units combining quarrelsome guerrilla factions and the white Rhodesian Army did not proceed without incident. White soldiers massacred their former enemies, and divisions among guerrilla groups caused renewed conflict. White farmers and technicians distrusted the government's guarantees, and thousands fled the country. Despite the strains, however, the government of Robert Mugabe brought peace to the country, revived the economy, and maintained close ties to the West. Problems exist, but they are the domestic difficulties of a new, independent country, not conflicts that threaten to involve the entire region of southern Africa.

The principal difference between El Salvador and

Zimbabwe is the attitude of the external actors. In El Salvador's case, they are the major obstacles to a negotiated solution. In Zimbabwe's case the principal backers of the Smith regime—Great Britain, the United States, and South Africa—and the most important supporters of the guerrillas—Angola, Mozambique, Zambia, Nigeria, Tanzania—all pressed hard for talks. They conditioned their support for a particular side on acceptance of the mediation process. In El Salvador, however, the principal backer of the Duarte regime—the United States—has resisted negotiation, as has the Salvadoran government's most important regional ally, Guatemala. This has made the Salvadoran High Command even more inflexible; they have no incentive to go to the bargaining table as long as military supply lines are not cut, and the guerrillas do not establish strongholds near the northern borders.

Duarte and the Christian Democrats indicated their willingness to enter into a dialogue as early as September, 1980; the Salvadoran military has not. Once, in February 1981, when Duarte was to fly to Bonn for talks with FDR President Guillermo Ungo, an attempted coup by the right kept the Salvadoran president in the capital.[239] In May 1981, when the Secretary General of the Socialist International, Hans Jürgen Wischnewski, visited Central America to look into the possibility of mediation, he found Duarte "open" to dialogue but Defense Minister García "skeptical" and the Army "determined to keep power in its own hands."[240] By the time Socialist International Vice-President Ed Broadbent visited San Salvador in June, Army commanders and the Reagan administration had convinced Duarte to change his position.[241] The Salvadoran president rejected the idea of a dialogue, and instead announced that the election campaign would soon get under way.

With the prospect of negotiation stalled in the short-run, the Reagan administration, by giving millions of dollars in aid to the Salvadoran military and infusing money into the failing—and insatiable—Salvadoran economy, could enable the government to prolong the war indefinitely. Reagan also could stage military action in the Caribbean or off the shores of Nicaragua or Cuba; the Reagan administration could continue supporting covert military activities against Nicaragua in order to stop what intelligence officials claim is a continued arms flow. But these actions will not end the war in El Salvador, and the country will continue to be a financial and moral burden on the United States.

The Reagan administration may long for the days when the United States sent gunboats steaming into Latin American harbors to ensure the installation of governments favorable to Washington. But the post-Vietnam decade appears to have placed limits on such a unilateralist policy. First, regional allies such as Venezuela, the strongest backer of the Duarte government after the United States, rejected U.S. military action in Central America in a message delivered to President Reagan by Venezuelan President Herrera Campins in November 1981.[242] Second, the Pentagon appears concerned that military action in Central America would divert U.S. military resources to the extent that more crucial positions—the Middle East, particularly—would be left vulnerable. Third and most important, large segments of the U.S. public and the Congress distrust the Reagan administration's characterization of the Salvadoran government and the nature of the conflict; Reagan has failed to persuade the American people that unqualified U.S. aid is warranted to help the Army defeat "leftist terrorists."

This, perhaps, may be the lesson of Vietnam as it relates to El Salvador—that the executive branch may not prefer a Salvadoran government that comprises revolutionaries, but can no longer convince Congress and the American public to pay the price to prevent it.* If the Reagan administration ultimately decides that armed intervention is the only way to avoid a "communist takeover," it will confront a populace that has been significantly

---

* In early March 1982, the House of Representatives voted 396-3 in favor of a resolution seeking "unconditional discussions" in El Salvador. On March 8, 1982 Senate Minority Leader Robert Byrd introduced legislation requiring authorization by Congress before any U.S. troops could be sent to El Salvador. Following the announcement of Mexican President López Portillo's peace proposal for Central America, 104 Congressmen, including twelve Republicans, wrote President Reagan asking that he support the initiative.

affected by a declining economy, and therefore is less willing to sustain a prolonged foreign adventure than it was during the Vietnam era.

Even if one accepts the Reagan administration's premise that the line must be drawn in El Salvador to prevent the spread of Soviet-sponsored "terrorism"—one must ask what it means to "win" there. Is it a victory for the United States to kill 200,000 civilians in an attempt to wipe out the guerrillas? Is it "resolve" to back a government that will remain unstable and indefinitely dependent on vast sums of U.S. economic and military aid? Is it reasonable to assume that any government in El Salvador—however chosen—can rule effectively without participation from the left? The Reagan administration has not taken these long-range questions into consideration while pursuing its limited short- and medium-range goals.

The failure to address these issues, and the resulting inability to find a solution to the Salvadoran crisis, is rooted in a distortion of the definition of U.S. national security. Since the onset of the Cold War and the policy of containment, U.S. policymakers have viewed the complex processes of postwar decolonization and development through a single, anti-Soviet prism. Movements for reform and wars of national liberation have been stripped of their historical foundations and their legitimacy. They have been seen only as extensions of Soviet power or as results of direct Soviet intervention and hence a threat to U.S. global interests.

The geopolitical strategists of the Reagan administration have described Central America as a row of dominoes already in the process of falling the wrong way. The Sandinista overthrow of Anastasio Somoza was the first domino that fell, and its effects will spread to El Salvador, then Guatemala, up through the oil fields of Mexico to the United States itself. The domino theory is simple and neat, but is nevertheless wholly irrelevant to the region. It is a metaphor drawn from physics and immutable natural law, and thus has little use in explaining social, evolutionary processes. It is true that events in one country have an impact on neighboring states, but conditions leading to revolution in El Salvador or stability in
90   Mexico are determined and sustained by local environments.

Thus, "curing" El Salvador of Marxism would do little to halt polarization in Guatemala, just as Mexican stability has not been threatened (indeed, it has been enhanced) by a political alliance with Salvadoran revolutionaries.

The domino theory and other national security concepts have another important flaw. They assume that the United States is essentially helpless to guide and determine its future, especially as it relates to relations with tiny Central American states. To a certain degree, the United States reaps what it sows in the hemisphere, and by pursuing a policy of unremitting hostility, contributes to the confirmation of its worst fears.

The cutoff of aid to Nicaragua, for example, has not substantially hurt the Sandinistas, but only forced them to turn—with success—to other sources for support. U.S. influence and prestige—especially with those sectors in Nicaragua that the United States ostensibly supports— have suffered as a consequence. Similarly, the Nicaraguan arms buildup so roundly condemned in Washington might be slowed by the dismantling of *Somocista* exile training camps in Miami, the termination of covert policies of destabilization, or the abandonment of rhetoric that threatens blockades and intervention.

Alternatives are available in Central America, but only on the condition that flexibility replace rigid Cold War thinking. A mature relationship with other nations in the hemisphere implies the ability—which European and important hemispheric powers possess—to deal with states having a wide variety of political systems and ideologies. It also implies recognition that underdeveloped countries need U.S. aid, technology, investment, and good will to pursue national development goals.

The alternative to accommodation of the left in Central America is continued conflict, years of instability, tens of thousands dead or homeless, and millions of dollars wasted. Central Americans during the last century have paid a heavy price for U.S. interference in the region. If the war in El Salvador continues, those costs—in terms of lives, treasure, and prestige—will be increasingly borne by the United States.

GLOSSARY

THE JUNTA: name given to four consecutive governments that have held power in El Salvador since October 15, 1979.

> *first Junta:* October 15, 1979-January 3, 1980—*Colonel Adolfo Arnoldo Majano* (Army), *Colonel Jaime Abdul Gutiérrez* (Army; made a General in January, 1982), *Román Mayorga Quirós* (rector of the Catholic University), *Guillermo Manuel Ungo* (Secretary General of the Social Democratic Party MNR), *Mario Andino* (private sector);

> *second Junta:* January 10, 1980-March 3, 1980— Colonel Majano, Colonel Gutiérrez, *Hector Dada Hirezi* (Christian Democrat), *José Antonio Morales Ehrlich* (Christian Democrat), *José Ramón Avalos Navarrete* (independent);

> *third Junta:* March 9, 1980-December 7, 1980— Colonel Majano, Colonel Gutiérrez, *José Napoleón Duarte* (Christian Democrat), Morales Ehrlich, Avalos Navarrete;

> *fourth Junta:* December 13, 1980-March 28, 1982— Duarte (President), Gutiérrez (Vice-president and Commander-in-Chief of the Armed Forces), Morales Ehrlich (head of the Agrarian Reform), Avalos Navarrete (head of social services).

THE MILITARY: the Army, Navy, and Air Force, numbering 12,000, and the security forces—the National Guard (4500 men headed by *General Carlos Eugenio Vides Casanova)*, the National Police (4500 men headed by *Colonel Carlos Reynaldo López Nuila)*, and the Treasury Police (2500 men headed by *Colonel Francisco Morán)*. All branches of the armed and security forces are under the jurisdiction of the Minister of Defense and Public Security, *General José Guillermo García.*

PARAMILITARY GROUPS:

> *ORDEN (Organización Democrática Nacionalista)* — civilian paramilitary network of 50,000-100,000

people under the direction of the President of the Republic, founded in 1968;

partrullas cantonales (rural patrols)—made up of former servicemen authorized to carry weapons; functions as a kind of army reserve;

death squads — White Warrior's Union (UGB), Escuadrón de la Muerte (EM), Maximiliano Hernández Martínez Brigades, Anti-Communist Armed Forces of Liberation—War of Extermination (FALANGE): right-wing terror units emerging in the mid- to late-1970s, operating with the acquiescence, if not direct collaboration, of government military forces.

POLITICAL PARTIES:

Christian Democratic Party (PDC)—founded in November 1960 on principles of social Christianity and private property; in power with the military since January 1980;

National Revolutionary Movement (MNR)—social democratic party founded in 1965; member of the Socialist International;

National Democratic Union (UDN)—founded in 1969; operated as the legal expression of the outlawed Communist Party;

National Opposition Union (UNO)—coalition of PDC, MNR, and UDN in 1972 and 1977 presidential elections.

PRIVATE SECTOR ORGANIZATIONS:

National Association of Private Enterprise (ANEP)— conservative association of 42 private sector organizations founded in the late 1960s and representing agro-export, commercial, and industrial interests. Important members include the Salvadoran Chamber of Commerce and the Salvadoran Association of Industry (ASI);

Productive Alliance (AP)—private sector association founded in 1980; dominated by industrial and commercial interests with little representation of land owners;

Eastern Region Farmers' Front (FARO)—land owners' association founded in late 1975 to block the Molina government's attempt at land reform.

POPULAR ORGANIZATIONS AND LEFT COALITONS:

Popular Revolutionary Bloc (BPR)—largest of the popular organizations, founded in 1975. Coalition of peasants, workers, students, teachers, and slum dwellers, including the two major peasant federations—the Federation of Christian Peasants (FECCAS) and the Union of Rural Workers (UTC)—the national teachers' organization (ANDES), the Union of Urban Dwellers (UPT), the Union Coordinating Committee (CCS), and three university and secondary school federations (MERS, FUR, and UR-19). Has links with the FPL;

United Popular Action Front (FAPU)—oldest of the popular organizations, founded in 1974. Member organizations include two student unions (FUERSA and ARDES), one peasant union (MRC), one labor union (VP), and one teachers' organization (OMR). Has links with the FARN;

Popular Leagues-28th of February (LP-28)—among the smallest of popular organizations, named after the 1977 massacre of demonstrators protesting General Carlos Humberto Romero's fraudulent election. Primarily student dominated, but has one union affiliate (LPO), one peasant league (LPC), and one association of market workers (ASUTRAMES). Linked to the ERP;

Popular Liberation Movement (MLP)—smallest of the popular organizations, founded in late 1979, and linked to the PRTC;

Revolutionary Coordinating Council of the Masses (CRM)—executive committee of popular organizations and the UDN formed in January 1980.

Democratic Front (FD)—alliance of union, professional, and university groups as well as the Social Democrats and a splinter of the Christian Democrats, formed in April 1980.

Revolutionary Democratic Front (FDR)—alliance of the popular organizations represented in the CRM with the 12 groups of the Democratic Front, founded in April 1980. First President of the FDR was *Enrique Alvarez Cordoba,* killed in November 1980, along with five other FDR leaders. Current president of the FDR is Secretary General of the MNR, *Guillermo Ungo.*

GUERRILLA GROUPS:

Popular Forces of Liberation (FPL)—largest of the guerrilla forces, founded in 1970, headed by *Salvador Cayetano Carpio,* former member of the Communist Party;

Peoples' Revolutionary Army (ERP)—guerrilla group founded by students and a radicalized splinter of the Christian Democrats in 1971, headed by *Joaquín Villalobos;*

Armed Forces of National Resistance (FARN)—guerrilla group found in 1975, out of a split with the ERP following the assassination of poet Roque Dalton; headed by *Fermán Cienfuegos;*

Communist Party of El Salvador (PCES)—party founded in 1930, but outlawed virtually since its founding; armed wing headed by *Schafik Jorge Handal;*

Revolutionary Party of Central American Workers (PRTC)—small armed group founded in 1979, headed by *Roberto Roca;*

Unified Revolutionary Directorate (DRU)—policy and strategy committee for all five guerrilla groups, first established in May 1980;

Farabundo Martí National Liberation Front (FMLN)—coalition of all five guerrilla groups, formed in October 1980.

FOOTNOTES

1. *The New York Times*, Feb. 19, 1982.

2. *The New York Times*, Feb. 20, 1982.

3. U.S. Department of State, "Communist Interference in El Salvador" (Bureau of Public Affairs, Washington, D.C.) Feb. 23, 1981, p. 1.

4. *The Washington Post*, March 3, 1982.

5. Testimony of Secretary of State Alexander Haig to the Senate Foreign Relations Committee, Feb. 2, 1982.

6. *The New York Times*, March 3, 1982.

7. *Newsweek*, March 1, 1982.

8. Amnesty International, "Amnesty International Newsletter Supplement," London, March, 1982.

9. Inter-American Development Bank, *Economic and Social Progress in Latin America* (Washington, D.C., 1979) p. 248.

10. International Commission of Jurists, *Review*, "El Salvador," June, 1978, p. 2.

11. David Browning, *El Salvador: La Tierra y El Hombre,* (Dirección de Publicaciones, Ministerio de Educación, San Salvador, El Salvador, 1975) p. 105.

12. *Ibid.*, p. 91.

13. Ralph Lee Woodward, Jr., *Central America : A Nation Divided* (Oxford University Press, New York, 1976) p. 91.

14. Browning, *op. cit.*, p. 241.

15. *Ibid.*, p. 249.

16. Cited in Laurence Simon and James Stephens, *El Salvador Land Reform 1980-81 : Impact Audit* (Oxfam America, Boston, 1981) p. 7.

17. *Ibid.*, p. 6.

18. *Latin America Regional Report*, March 21, 1980.

19. *The New York Times*, Feb. 20, 1981.

20. Testimony of Assistant Secretary of State for Inter-American Affairs Thomas O. Enders before the House Appropriations Subcommittee on Foreign Operations, Feb. 1, 1982, p. 3.

21. Interview, U.S. Department of State, Oct. 17, 1979.

22. Testimony of Assistant Secretary of State for Inter-American Affairs Viron P. Vaky before the House Foreign Affairs Subcommittee on Inter-American Affairs, Sept. 11, 1979, pp. 1 and 4.

23. *The Washington Post,* Aug. 24, 1979.

24. Browning, *op. cit.,* p. 337.

25. *Ibid.,* p. 341.

26. *Ibid.,* p. 357.

27. *Ibid.,* p. 357.

28. Howard Blutstein, ed., *Area Handbook on El Salvador* (U.S. Government Printing Office, Washington, D.C., 1971) p. 195.

29. *Ibid.,* p. 195.

30. Rodolfo Barón Castro, *La Población de El Salvador* (Universidad Católica José Simeón Cañas, San Salvador, El Salvador).

31. Thomas Anderson, *Matanza: El Salvador's Communist Revolt of 1932* (University of Nebraska Press, Lincoln, Neb., 1971) p. 10.

32. Browning, *op. cit.,* p. 365.

33. Anderson, *op. cit.,* p. 83.

34. *Ibid.,* p. 25.

35. *Ibid.,* p. 26.

36. Mario Menendez Rodriguez, *El Salvador: Una Autentica Guerra Civil* (Editorial Universitaria Centroamericana, 1980) p. 150.

37. Anderson, *op. cit.,* p. 37.

38. Fernando Flores Pinel, "El Estado de Seguridad Nacional en El Salvador," in *Centroamérica en Crisis* (Centro de Estudios Internacionales, El Colegio de Mexico, Mexico, 1980) p. 70.

39. Roque Dalton, "Filosofia Para Gobernar El Salvador Por Periodos No Mayores (Ni Menores) de Trece Años," *Las Historias Prohibidas del Pulgarcito* (Siglo Veintiuno, Mexico, 1974) p. 125.

40. See Anderson, *op. cit.*

41. Stephen Webre, *José Napoleón Duarte and the Christian Democratic Party in Salvadoran Politics, 1960-1972* (Louisiana State University Press, Baton Rouge, 1979) p. 11.

42. *Ibid.,* p. 14.

43. Paul P. Kennedy, *The Middle Beat* (Teachers' College Press, Columbia University, New York, 1971) p. 172.

44. Robert Armstrong, *El Salvador - Why Revolution?* (North American Congress on Latin America, New York, March - April, 1980) p. 8.

45. *Ibid.,* p. 10.

46. Webre, *op. cit.,* p. 29.

47. Ibid., p. 26.

48. *Ibid.,* p. 32.

49. *Ibid.,* p. 37.

50. Quoted in Anderson, *op. cit.*, p. 157.

51. Webre, *op. cit.*, p. 51.

52. *The Philadelphia Inquirer*, Nov. 29, 1961.

53. Armstrong, *op. cit.*, p. 11.

54. *Ibid.*, p. 11.

55. Webre, *op. cit.*, p. 72.

56. Armstrong, *op. cit.*, p. 11.

57. U.S. Agency for International Development, *Termination Phase-Out Study, Public Safety Project, El Salvador* (Washington, D.C., 1974) pp. 9, 13.

58. U.S. Agency for International Development, Office of Public Safety, *Report on Visit to Central America and Panama* (Washington, D.C., 1967) p. 8.

59. *Ibid.*, p. 23.

60. Webre, *op. cit.*, p. 102.

61. Kennedy, *op. cit.*, p. 184.

62. Murat Williams, letter to the author, March 28, 1980.

63. David R. Raynolds, *Rapid Development in Small Economies: The Example of El Salvador* (Praeger Publishers, New York, 1967) p. 1.

64. Webre, *op. cit*, p. 110.

65. *Ibid.*, p. 136.

66. Flores Pinel, *op. cit.*, p. 77.

67. Raynolds, *op. cit.*, p. 20.

68. Rafael Guidos Vejar, "La Crisis Política en El Salvador," *Estudios Centroamericanos*, Julio-Agosto 1979, p. 511.

69. Webre, *op. cit.*, p. 153.

70. *Ibid.*, p. 163.

71. *Ibid.*, p. 170.

72. Quoted in Webre, *Ibid.*, p. 171.

73. U.S. Congress, House International Relations Committee, Hearings, *Human Rights in Nicaragua, Guatemala, and El Salvador: Implications for U.S. Policy,* 94th Cong., 2nd sess. (U.S. Government Printing Office, Washington, D.C., 1976) p. 43.

74. César Jerez, "The Church in Central America," *New Catholic World*, Sept-Oct. 1981, p. 197.

75. *Ibid.*, p. 197.

76. Quoted in Philip Berryman, "What Happened at Puebla," in Levine, ed., *Churches and Politics in Latin America* (Sage Publications, Beverly Hills, 1979) p. 84.

77. Penny Lernoux, *Cry of the People* (Doubleday and Co., New York, 1980) p. 70.

78. *Ibid.*, p. 70.

79. *Estudios Centroamericanos*, San Salvador, Jan.-Feb. 1972.

80. U.S. Agency for International Development, Office of Public Safety, *op. cit.*, p. 24.

81. Menéndez Rodríguez, *op. cit.*, p. 26.

82. *Ibid.*, p. 120.

83. *Ibid.*, p. 182.

84. U.S. Congress, House International Relations Subcommittee on International Organizations and on Inter-American Affairs, Hearings, *The Recent Presidential Elections in El Salvador : Implications for U.S. Foreign Policy*, 95th Cong., 1st sess. (U.S. Government Printing Office, Washington, D.C., 1977) p. 50.

85. U.S. Congress, House International Relations Committee, 1976, *op. cit.*, p. 83.

86. Lernoux, *op. cit.*, p. 72.

87. U.S. Congress, House International Relations Committee, 1976, *op. cit.*, p. 167.

88. *Ibid.*, p. 44.

89. *Ibid.*, p. 44.

90. Interview, Washington, D.C., July 9, 1981.

91. U.S. Congress, House International Relations Committee, 1976, *op. cit.*, p. 46.

92. Lernoux, *op. cit.*, p. 68.

93. Menéndez Rodríguez, *op. cit.*, p. 105.

94. Webre, *op. cit.*, p. 196.

95. U.S. Congress, House International Relations Subcommittees on International Organizations and on Inter-American Affairs, *op. cit*, p. 53.

96. Organization of American States, Inter-American Commission on Human Rights, *Report on the Situation of Human Rights in El Salvador* (OAS, Washington, D.C., 1978) p. 54.

97. Webre, *op. cit.*, p. 198.

98. U.S. Congress, House International Relations Subcommittees on International Organizations and on Inter-American Affairs, *op. cit*, p. 4.

99. *Ibid.*, p. 50.

100. International Commission of Jurists, *op. cit.* p. 2.

101. Lernoux, *op. cit.*, p. 74.

102. *Ibid.*, p. 76.

103. Rafael Guidos Vejar, *op. cit.*, p. 518.

104. *Ibid.*, p. 519.

105. *Ibid.*, p. 510.

106. *Ibid.*, p. 511.

107. *The Washington Post*, May 9, 1979.

108. "Plataforma Comun del Foro Popular" (San Salvador, El Salvador) Sept. 1979.

109. *The Washington Post*, Oct. 17, 1979.

110. *The Washington Post*, Aug. 2, 1979.

111. *The New York Times*, Sept. 14, 1979.

112. *The New York Times*, Oct. 19, 1979.

113. "Proclama de la Fuerza Armada de la Republica de El Salvador" (Publicaciones de la Secretaria de Informacion de la Presidencia de la Republica, San Salvador, El Salvador) Oct. 15, 1979.

114. *Ibid.*, pp. 3-4.

115. Carolyn Forché, "The Road to Reaction in El Salvador," *The Nation*, June 14, 1980, p. 713.

116. Interview, Roman Mayorga, Washington, D.C., Nov. 2, 1981.

117. Interviews with junta and Cabinet members serving in the first junta, June-Sept., 1981.

118. Amnesty International, "Update on El Salvador," London, Dec. 11, 1979.

119. Quoted in Marcel Salamín, *El Salvador: Sin Piso y Sin Techo* (Panama, 1980) p. 33.

120. *The New York Times*, Oct. 27, 1981.

121. Report of the special investigative commission on political prisoners and disappeared persons, *Estudios Centroamericanos*, Jan. - Feb. 1980, pp. 136-139.

122. Interviews, former Salvadoran soldiers and military officers, Washington, D.C., July 1981.

123. Salamín, *op. cit.*, p. 36.

124. Interview, Capt. Ricardo Alejandro Fiallos, Washington, D.C., April 30, 1981.

125. Interview, Román Mayorga, Washington, D.C., Nov. 2, 1981.

126. Documents received by the author from the Department of Defense under the Freedom of Information Act.

127. Planteamiento de Miembros del Gabinete a la Junta Revolucionaria de Gobierno" (San Salvador, El Salvador) Dec. 7, 1979, p. 3.

128. Salamín, *op. cit.*, p. 31.

129. Interviews, junta and Cabinet members of the first junta, June-Sept., 1981.

130. COPEFA, "Al Pueblo Salvadoreño y a Los Señores Ministros, Subsecretarios y Demas Funcionarios que Suscribieron el Documento Dirigido a la Fuerza Armada" (San Salvador, El Salvador) Jan. 2, 1980.

131. Interview, U.S. Department of State, Jan. 10, 1980.

132. Letter of resignation of Guillermo Ungo and Roman Mayorga (San Salvador, El Salvador) Jan. 3, 1980, p. 2.

133. Letter of resignation to junta from the Cabinet (San Salvador, El Salvador) Jan. 3, 1980, p. 2.

134. Interview, member of the MNR, Washington, D.C., July 21, 1981.

135. *The Washington Post,* Jan. 23, 1980; American Civil Liberties Union, *Report on Human Rights in El Salvador* (Washington, D.C., Jan. 1980) p. 31.

136. See also Tommie Sue Montgomery, "U.S. Policy and the Revolutionary Process: The Case of El Salvador," unpublished manuscript, May 1980, p. 7.

137. Hector Dada Hirezi, "Why the Christian Democrats of El Salvador Abandoned the Government and their Party," presentation to Permanent People's Tribunal, Mexico City, Feb. 10, 1981 (distributed by EPICA, Washington, D.C.) pp. 10-11.

138. *Ibid.*, pp. 13-14.

139. Letter of resignation of Hector Dada Hirezi (San Salvador, El Salvador) March 3, 1980, p. 1.

140. Interview, Col. Eldon Cummings, San Salvador, July 14, 1980.

141. See testimony of John A. Bushnell, U.S. Congress House Appropriations Subcommittee on Foreign Operations, Hearings, *Foreign Assistance and Related Programs Appropriations for 1981,* 96th Cong., 2nd sess. (U.S. Government Printing Office, Washington, D.C. 1980) pp. 324-335.

142. Testimony of Franklin D. Kramer, *Ibid.*, p. 340.

143. See letter of resignation of Christian Democratic Party leaders from the Christian Democratic Party, March 10, 1980.

144. Amnesty International, "News Release," New York, March 17, 1980.

145. See letter of resignation of Under Secretary of Agriculture Jorge Villacorta, *El Independiente,* March 29, 1980.

146. Quoted in *Foreign Broadcast Information Service*, (hereinafter cited as *FBIS)* March 11, 1980.

147. See footnote 143.

148. U.S. Agency for International Development, "Agrarian Reform Organization, Annex IIA: A Social Analysis," Washington, D.C., June 1980, p. 20.

149. March 23, 1980 homily of Archbishop Oscar Romero, reprinted in *Sojourners*, May 1980, pp. 12-16.

150. Quoted in Menéndez Rodríguez, *op. cit.*, p. 105.

151. Testimony of Robert White, U.S. Senate Committee on Foreign Relations, Hearings, *The Situation in El Salvador*, 97th Cong., 1st sess. (U.S. Government Printing Office, Washington, D.C., 1981) p. 117.

152. Interview, aide to Rep. Matthew McHugh (D-NY), April 1, 1980.

153. Quoted in *FBIS*, April 8, 1980.

154. Quoted in Robert Armstrong and Janet Shenk, *El Salvador - A Revolution Brews* (North American Congress on Latin America, New York, July-Aug. 1980) pp. 31-32.

155. Quoted in *FBIS*, April 25, 1980.

156. Quoted in Armstrong and Shenk, *op. cit.*, p. 25.

157. *Diario Las Américas*, May 11, 1980.

158. *FBIS*, May 15, 1980.

159. *FBIS*, May 13, 1980.

160. Legal Aid Service of the Archdiocese of San Salvador, *El Salvador - One Year of Repression* (World Council of Churches, Geneva, 1981) p. 13.

161. *Latin America Weekly Report*, Aug. 22, 1980.

162. *FBIS*, Sept. 19, 1980.

163. *Latin America Weekly Report*, Sept. 26, 1980.

164. UPI, Sept. 22, 1980.

165. Quoted in *FBIS*, Oct. 31, 1980.

166. Interview, San Salvador, July 21, 1980.

167. Interview, FDR representative, Washington, D.C., Aug. 1980.

168. Quoted in Armstrong and Shenk, *op. cit.*, p. 24.

169. Legal Aid Service of the Archdiocese of San Salvador, *op. cit.*, p. 16.

170. Speech by Ronald Reagan, "Peace and Security in the 1980's," Chicago, Illinois, March 17, 1980.

171. *The New York Times*, Nov. 29, 1980.

172. Pedro A. Sanjuan, "Interim Report on the Bureau on Inter-American Affairs and Related Bureaus and Policy Areas, Department of State," Washington, D.C., 1980.

173. Telephone interview, Marie Rieckleman, May 5, 1981.

174. *Los Angeles Times*, July 8, 1981 (article by John Dinges for Pacific News Service).

175. U.S. Department of State, "Press Release," Dec. 5, 1980.

176. Quoted in *The New York Times*, Dec. 7, 1980.

177. *FBIS*, Dec. 11, 1980.

178. UPI, Dec. 14, 1980.

179. U.S. Department of State, "Press Release," Dec. 17, 1980.

180. *Cleveland Press*, Nov. 15, 1981; *Cleveland Plain Dealer*, Nov. 14, 1981; and interview, office of Rep. Mary Rose Oakar, Dec. 5, 1981.

181. See testimony of Leonel Gómez, U.S. Congress House Appropriations Subcommittee on Foreign Operations, Hearings, *Foreign Assistance and Related Programs Appropriations for 1982*, 97th Cong., 1st sess. (U.S. Government Printing Office, Washington, D.C., 1981) p. 353.

182. *The Washington Post*, Dec. 27, 1980.

183. U.S. Department of State, "Press Release, " Jan. 14, 1981.

184. *The New York Times*, Jan. 19, 1981.

185. *The New York Times*, Jan. 15, 1981.

186. *The Washington Post*, Jan. 15, 1981.

187. Testimony of Robert White, U.S. Senate Committee on Foreign Relations, *op. cit.*, pp. 100-164.

188. U.S. Department of State, "Press Release," Jan. 17, 1981.

189. *The New York Times*, Feb. 21, 1981.

190. Testimony of Alexander Haig before the House Foreign Affairs Committee, March 18, 1981.

191. *The Boston Globe*, Feb. 1, 1981.

192. *The New York Times*, Feb. 21, 1981.

193. *The Washington Post*, Feb. 22, 1981.

194. U.S. Department of State, "Press Release," March 2, 1981.

195. *The Washington Post*, Feb. 27, 1981; *The New York Times*, Feb. 26, 1981 and March 12, 1981.

196. *The Washington Post*, March 27, 1981.

197. Testimony of Archbishop Joseph Hickey, U.S. Congress House Foreign Affairs Subcommittee on Inter-American Affairs, Hearings, *U.S. Policy Toward El Salvador*, 97th Cong., 1st sess. (U.S. Government Printing Office, Washington, D.C., 1981) p. 53.

198. *The Washington Post*, March 13, 1981.

199. Testimony of John A. Bushnell, House Foreign Affairs Subcommittee on Inter-American Affairs, March 23, 1981.

200. *The New York Times*, Feb. 24, 1981 and March 12, 1981.

201. John Dinges, Pacific News Service, in *The Los Angeles Times*, March 17, 1981.

202. *The Wall Street Journal*, June 8, 1981.

203. *The Washington Post*, May 16, 1981.

204. The White House, "Determination to Authorize Continued Assistance for El Salvador" (Presidential Determination No. 82-4) Jan. 28, 1982.

205. Amnesty International, "News Release," New York, Feb. 9, 1982.

206. Speech by Thomas O. Enders, "El Salvador: The Search for Peace," World Affairs Council, Washington, D.C., July 16, 1981.

207. *The Washington Post*, June 27, 1981.

208. Figures based on Salvadoran government and U.S. Embassy sources, as cited in *The Boston Globe*, Aug. 19, 1981; EFE, May 10, 1981, and Jan. 27, 1982; UPI, June 11, 1981.

209. Speech by Deane R. Hinton before the American Chamber of Commerce, San Salvador, July 31, 1981, p. 1.

210. Memorandum to Pres. José Napoleón Duarte from the Union Comunal Salvadorena (UCS), Dec. 10, 1981.

211. *The New York Times*, Jan. 26, 1982.

212. *The New York Times*, Aug. 29, 1981.

213. "Declaration of Nine Latin American Countries with Regard to the Recognition of Leftist Guerrilla Groups of El Salvador, By the Governments of Mexico and France," Caracas, Venezuela, Sept. 2, 1981.

214. *Time*, Sept. 7, 1981.

215. Quoted in *The Washington Post*, Oct. 30, 1981.

216. Testimony of Alexander Haig before the House Foreign Affairs Committee, Nov. 12, 1981.

217. U.S. Department of State, "Cuba's Renewed Support for Violence in the Hemisphere" (research paper presented to the Senate Foreign Relations Committee, Subcommittee on Western Hemisphere Affairs) Dec. 14, 1981.

218. *FBIS*, Oct. 22, 1981.

219. *FBIS*, Oct. 21, 1981.

220. Testimony of Thomas O. Enders before the Senate Foreign Relations Committee, Dec. 14, 1981.

221. Testimony of Fred Ikle before the Senate Foreign Relations Committee, Dec. 15, 1981.

222. *The New York Times*, Dec. 3, 1981.

223. *FBIS*, Jan. 19, 1982.

224. *The Washington Post*, March 10, 1982. See also Saul Landau and Craig Nelson, "The CIA Rides Again," *The Nation*, March 6, 1982.

225. ABC News, March 11, 1982.

226. *The New York Times*, March 11, 1982.

227. See footnote 20.

228. *The Washington Post*, Jan. 31, 1982.

229. *Aviation Week and Space Technology*, Feb. 8, 1982.

230. Question by Sen. Nancy Kassenbaum (R-KN) to Assistant Secretary of State for Inter-American Affairs Thomas Enders, Senate Foreign Relations Committee, Hearings, Feb. 8, 1982.

231. Testimony of Enders, *Ibid.*

232. Sunday homily of Salvadoran Apostolic Administator Arturo Rivera y Damas, San Salvador, Jan. 3, 1982.

233. Enders speech before the World Affairs Council, *op. cit.*, p. 5.

234. Frente Democrático Revolucionario, "Position of the FDR-FMLN's Political - Diplomatic Commission on Elections and Political Solutions," El Salvador, July 22, 1981, pp. 5-6.

235. Reprinted in *FBIS*, April 1, 1981.

236. Speech by Daniel Ortega before the United Nations General Assembly, Oct. 7, 1981, pp. 28-30.

237. *The New York Times*, Jan. 28, 1982.

238. *The Washington Post*, Feb. 22, 1982.

239. *The New York Times*, March 5, 1981.

240. "Central America Watch," *The Nation*, July 11-18, 1981.

241. *The Toronto Star*, June 11, 1981.

242. *The Washington Post*, Nov. 18, 1981.

APPENDIX I

U.S. ECONOMIC AND MILITARY AID TO EL SALVADOR (in thousands of $)

U.S. Fiscal Year	1979	1980	1981	1982 (est.)	1982* (supp.)	1983 (proposed)
Economic Aid						
Economic Support Funds	—	9,100	44,900	40,000	128,000	105,000
Development Assistance	6,045	43,155	33,300	35,000	—	25,000
P.L. 480 Title I+	—	3,000	17,200	22,400	—	30,000
P.L. 480 Title II	2,573	3,269	9,100	7,100	—	4,900
Housing Investment Guaranty	—	9,500	5,500	15,000	—	—
Commodity Credit Corporation	—	4,000	27,045	24,800	—	—
Total	8,618	72,024	136,514	144,278	128,000	164,921
Military Aid						
Foreign Military Sales	—	5,947	10,000	16,500	—	60,000
Military Assistance Program	—	8	3	8,500	35,000	—
Training	—	300	492	1,000	—	1,300
Section 506 FAA**	—	—	25,000	55,000	—	—
Total	—	6,255	35,495	81,000	35,000	61,300
TOTAL ECONOMIC AND MILITARY	8,618	78,279	172,009	225,278	163,000	226,221

* part of President Reagan's Caribbean Initiative, supplemental appropriation

+ Food for Peace program

** Emergency powers granted to the President under Section 506 of the Foreign Assistance Act to provide military assistance in case of "an unforeseen emergency."

Source: U.S. Department of State, March 22, 1980.

APPENDIX II

U.S. MILITARY PERSONNEL IN EL SALVADOR, MARCH 1981*

6— Staff of U.S. Military Group at the Embassy in San Salvador (raised from a level of 4), to serve as a liaison with the Salvadoran armed forces and gather military intelligence;

14— training in the use of and maintenance of helicopters;

6— naval training team to "assist the Salvadoran Navy in improving its capability to interdict seaborne infiltration of arms destined for the leftist guerrillas and to survey the need for upgrading and refurbishing Salvadoran patrol boats and provide training in the maintenance of boats and other naval equipment." The team left the port of La Unión in mid-April, and was subsequently replaced by a smaller team of 3;

5— augment the Military Group for administrative and logistics purposes related to the presence of additional U.S. personnel;

5— Operational Planning and Assistance Team (OPAT) to assist each of El Salvador's five regional commands in the planning and improvement of intelligence, communications, and logistics, and to serve as a liaison between regional and national commands;

5— Operational Planning and Assistance Team to work with senior Army commanders at the headquarters

---

* Information for the list comes from a variety of different sources, including documents received by the author under the Freedom of Information Act; interviews, U.S. Department of State and Department of Defense; *The New York Times*, March 1, 10, 14, 29, and July 8, 13, 1981; *The Washington Post*, March 3, 10, 18, and June 7, 1981; *The Los Angeles Times*, June 7, 1981; *The Washington Star*, February 24, 1981; *The Baltimore Sun*, February 3, 1981. Where information has been contradictory, author has relied on Administration sources. **107**

in San Salvador to establish communications links and coordination between army units in the five military districts;

15— three small unit training teams of five men each to "provide in-garrison training for the Salvadoran's new quick-reaction force." The 15 were counterinsurgency specialists from the Special Forces. They provided training in patrolling, air mobile operations, individual soldier skills, and counter-guerrilla operations. The "quick reaction force"— named the Atlacatl Battalion after a Salvadoran Indian chief—involves an infantry unit of 2000 men supported by helicopters for rapid mobility to points of conflict.

SUGGESTED BIBLIOGRAPHY

Books Available in English

American Civil Liberties Union and Americas Watch, *Human Rights in El Salvador*, New York: Vintage Press, 1982.

Anderson, Thomas, *Matanza: El Salvador's Communist Revolt of 1932*, Lincoln, Nebraska: University of Nebraska Press, 1971.

Armstrong, Robert, *El Savador—Why Revolution?* New York: North American Congress on Latin America, March-April, 1980.

——— and Janet Shenk, *El Salvador - A Revolution Brews*, New York: North American Congress on Latin America, July-August, 1980.

——————*El Salvador: The Face of Revolution*, Boston: South End Press, 1982.

Browning, David, *El Salvador - Landscape and Society*, London: Oxford University Press, 1971.

CAMINO, *El Salvador - Background to the Crisis*, Boston: Central America Information Office, 1982.

Erdozaín, Plácido, *Archbishop Romero: Martyr of El Salvador*, Maryknoll, N.Y.: Orbis Books, 1980.

Feinberg, Richard, ed., *Central America: International Dimensions of the Crisis*, New York: Holmes and Meier, 1982.

Gettleman, Marvin E., et al., *El Salvador: Central America in the New Cold War*, New York: Grove Press, 1981.

Legal Aid Service of the Archdiocese of San Salvador, *El Salvador - One Year of Repression*, Commission of the Churches on International Affairs, World Council of Churches, Geneva, 1981.

Lernoux, Penny, *Cry of the People*, New York: Penguin Books, 1980.

MacLeod, Murdo J., *Spanish Central America*, Berkeley, California: University of California Press, 1973.

Montgomery, Tommie Sue, *Revolution in El Salvador*, Boulder, Colorado: Westview Press, 1982.

Raynolds, David R., *Rapid Development in Small Economies: The Case of El Salvador*, New York: Praeger Publishers, 1967.

Simon, Laurence and James Stephens, *El Salvador Land Reform 1980-81: Impact Audit*, Boston: Oxfam America, Inc., 1981.

Webre, Stephen, *José Napoleón Duarte and the Christian Democratic Party in Salvadoran Politics 1960-1972,* Baton Rouge: Louisiana State University Press, 1979.

White, Alastair, *El Salvador,* New York: Praeger Publishers, 1973.

Woodward, Ralph Lee, Jr., *Central America - A Nation Divided,* New York: Oxford University Press, 1976.

Articles, Monographs, and Background Papers

Arnson, Cynthia, "Background Information on El Salvador and U.S. Military Assistance to Central America", Updates 1-6, Institute for Policy Studies *Resource,* Washington, D.C., Jan. 1980-March 1982.

Bonner, Raymond, "El Salvador - A Nation at War with Itself," *The New York Times Magazine,* Feb. 22, 1982.

Burbach, Roger, "Central America: The End of U.S. Hegemony? *Monthly Review,* Vol. 33, No. 8, Jan. 1982.

Christianity and Crisis, "Central America: A Season of Martyrs," Vol. 40, No. 8, May 12, 1980.

DiGiovanni, Cleto, "U.S. Policy and the Marxist Threat to Central America," *Heritage Foundation Backgrounder,* Washington, D.C., Oct. 15, 1980.

Committee of Santa Fe, "A New Inter-American Policy for the Eighties," Council for Inter-American Security, 1980.

Domínguez, Jorge, "U.S. Interests and Policies in the Caribbean and Central America," American Enterprise Institute *Special Analysis,* No. 81-9, Washington, D.C., 1982.

Fontaine, Roger, "Castro's Specter," *The Washington Quarterly,* Autumn, 1980.

Foreign Policy, "Struggle in Central America," No. 43, Summer, 1981 (Five articles by Leonel Gómez and Bruce Cameron, W. Scott Thompson, J. Bryan Hehir, Olga Pellicer, Marlise Simons).

Gleijeses, Piero, "Tilting at Windmills: Reagan in Central America," Caribbean Basin Program of The Johns Hopkins University School of Advanced International Studies, Washington, D.C., Spring, 1982.

Hoeffel, Paul, "The Eclipse of the Oligarchs," *The New York Times Magazine,* Sept. 6, 1981.

Kinzer, Stephen, "Central America: In Search of its Destiny," *The Boston Globe Magazine,* Aug. 16, 1981.

Kirkpatrick, Jeane, "Dictatorships and Double Standards," *Commentary,* Nov. 1979.

————, "U.S. Security and Latin America," *Commentary*, Jan. 1981.

Leiken, Robert, "Eastern Winds in Latin America," *Foreign Policy*, No. 42, Spring, 1981.

LeoGrande, William, "A Splendid Little War: Drawing the Line in El Salvador," *International Security*, Vol., 6, No. 1, Summer, 1981.
————and Robbins, Carla, "Oligarchs and Officers: The Crisis in El Salvador," *Foreign Affairs*, Summer, 1980.

Menges, Constantine, "Central American Revolutions: A New Dimension of Political Warfare," in the Eighth National Security Affairs Conference Proceedings, *The 1980s: Decade of Confrontation*, Fort Lesley J. McNair: National Defense University Press, 1981.

Montgomery, Tommie Sue, "El Salvador: The Descent into Violence," Center for International Policy *Report*, Washington, D.C., March, 1982.

Navarro, Vicente, "Genocide in El Salvador," *Monthly Review*, Vol. 32, No. 11, April, 1981.

New Catholic World, "The Church in Central America," Vol. 224, No. 1343, Sept.-Oct., 1981.

LIST OF
ORGANIZATIONS

American Civil Liberties Union
122 Maryland Ave., N.E.
Washington, D.C. 20002

American Enterprise Institute
1150 17th St., N.W.
Washington, D.C. 20036

American Friends Service Committee, NARMIC
1501 Cherry St.
Philadelphia, PA. 19102

American Security Council
499 South Capitol St., S.W.
Washington, D.C. 20003

Americas Watch
36 West 44th St.
New York, N.Y. 10036

Amnesty International
304 West 58th St.
New York, N.Y. 10019

Central America Information Office
1151 Massachusetts Ave.
Cambridge, MA. 02138

Center for International Policy
120 Maryland Ave., N.E.
Washington, D.C. 20002

CISPES
P.O. Box 12056
Washington, D.C. 20005

Coalition for a New Foreign and Military Policy
120 Maryland Ave., N.E.
Washington, D.C. 20002

Council for Inter-American Security
729 8th St., S.E.
Washington, D.C. 20003

Council on Hemispheric Affairs
1900 L St., N.W.
Washington, D.C. 20036

EPICA
1470 Irving St., N.W.
Washington, D.C. 20010

Heritage Foundation
513 C St., N.E.
Washington, D.C. 20002

Institute for Food and Development Policy
2588 Mission St.
San Francisco, CA. 94110

International Commission of Jurists
P.O. Box 120
109 route de Chêne
1224 Chêne-Bougeries
Geneva, Switzerland

Inter-Relgious Task Force on El Salvador
1747 Connecticut Ave., N.W.
Washington, D.C. 20009

NACLA
151 West 19th St.
New York, N.Y. 10011

OAS Inter-American Human Rights Commission
Constitution Ave. and 19th St., N.W.
First Floor
Washington, D.C. 20006

OXFAM America
115 Broadway
Boston, MA. 02116

Washington Office on Latin America
120 Maryland Ave., N.E.
Washington, D.C. 20002

Woodrow Wilson International Center for Scholars
1000 Jefferson Dr., S.W.
Washington, D.C. 20560

EPILOGUE
After The Elections

On March 28, 1982 1.4 million Salvadorans, about two thirds of the country's registered voters, went to the polls to elect representatives to a Constituent Assembly. Elated by the turn-out, Secretary of State Alexander Haig claimed the next day that "the Salvadoran people's stunning commitment to the power of the democratic vision is an unanswerable repudiation of the advocates of force and violence."[243] His sentiments were echoed by Deputy Assistant Secretary of State Everett Briggs, part of the U.S. election observer team. "I find words fail me," Briggs told the Senate Foreign Relations Committee on April 1, "to express the depth of the emotional impact that this event made on me."[244]

The United States government as well as the Salvadoran right have concluded that the elections were an accurate reflection of the will of the Salvadoran people, and a stunning blow to the guerrilla cause. They have thus attached a definitiveness to the voting results which may not be warranted by the circumstances. Elections in El Salvador, like all elections, must be judged in the context of the conditions that surround them. In El Salvador the immediate context was one of civil war and the suspension of constitutional guarantees.* In both the past and present, the very act of participating in elections has often signified for Salvadoran citizens little more than a way to avoid making enemies of the government.

El Salvador's new Constituent Assembly has the power to draw up a new constitution, appoint a provisional government to replace the junta led by José Napoleón Duarte, and set a date for a presidential election, probably in 1983. The Christian Democratic Party won the single largest share — 40.7 percent — of the valid votes cast on

---

* Certain rights suspended under a state of siege enacted in March 1980, such as the freedom of assembly and of the press, were reinstated during the election campaign, but in practice were extended only to registered parties and their affiliated political groups.

March 28. They are in minority, however, against a loose grouping of five right-wing parties, who together hold 36 seats in the Assembly against the Christian Democrats' 24. Of the parties of the right, the Nationalist Republican Alliance (ARENA), led by ex-Major Roberto D'Aubuisson, made the strongest show with 29.6 percent of valid votes. ARENA was followed closely by the National Conciliation Party (PCN), the party of the military, with 19.2 percent.

The March 28 elections undeniably altered the face of Salvadoran politics. The structure of power, however, remained largely unchanged. If anything, ARENA's share of the vote testified to the continued political clout of the oligarchy and those segments of the population who perceive their interests to be dependent on it. The military continued to be the ultimate arbiter of power, especially as military solutions to the problems of national security were embraced even tighter by dominant political coalitions.

Almost immediately after the election results were known, the parties of the right began clamoring for Duarte's ouster as president; the Christian Democrats, whose presence in the Salvadoran government had proved essential to U.S. support, wavered between accepting a limited role in the evolving government or going into opposition. On their fate rested the future—if only on paper—of the agrarian and commercial reforms that had also provided key elements of the government's legitimacy. Most important, the prospects for some form of dialogue with the left to end the war evaporated completely in the new circumstances. D'Aubuisson, who had promised during the campaign to "exterminate the subversives within three months" vowed once again to complete the effort in "no more than six."[245] The Salvadoran elections, by stripping power from the Christian Democrats, promised to intensify the fighting by marginalizing a key force in the search for a political solution.

In addition to the above observations, other serious questions must be raised about the conduct of the elections and the conclusiveness of their results:

- Only 1.4 million voters out of an estimated 2.2 million people who are old enough to vote went to the polls. **115**

(The Salvadoran population is 4.5 million.) This means that about 60 percent of eligible voters participated. (Of those who did vote, 11-13 percent cast blank or null ballots, further reducing effective participation.[246]

- Sixty percent of the turnout was in only 4 of El Salvador's 14 provinces (San Salvador, Santa Ana, La Libertad and Sonsonate). There was little voting in guerrilla controlled zones. (Chalatenango, Morazán and Usulutan together accounted for only 9.6 percent of the vote.) In 65 out of El Salvador's 261 municipalities, there was no voting at all.

- Assessing the motivation of the electorate is difficult if not impossible. While many surely voted out of clear preference for a certain party, others may have voted simply out of fear of the consequences of not voting. When voters cast their ballots, electoral officials recorded the number of the voter's I.D. card, thus providing Salvadoran officials with a central register of those who did (and did not) participate.

- Only one candidate, ex-Major D'Aubuisson, conducted a campaign throughout the country. The Christian Democrats and others declined to travel for reasons of security. (D'Aubuisson himself was wounded in an assassination attempt shortly before the election.)

- The opposition FMLN-FDR did not participate in the electoral process because they maintained that there were no conditions for free elections.* Although their share of the votes had they participated is difficult to estimate, the example of Zimbabwe may be illustrative: a national election in Zimbabwe in April 1979 as part of an "internal settlement" that excluded the guerrillas resulted in the victory of Bishop Abel Muzorewa, who captured 67 percent of valid votes. Ten months later, after international negotiations that facilitated the left's participation, Muzorewa's share declined to 8.2 percent while guerrilla leader Robert Mugabe won a clear majority.[247]

---

* The left announced a major new offensive for the time of the elections which it subsequently called off. There was, however, substantial military activity in areas of previous guerrilla actions.

In the post-election jockeying, the United States will play a key, if not decisive role. President Reagan acknowledged on March 31 that the emergence of a right-wing, anti-reform government in El Salvador would cause "great difficulties"[248] for the United States, because of the public and congressional reaction. Simultaneously, however, top administration officials began to tone down their assessment of the Salvadoran right in an attempt to soften its image. "The parties to the right of the Christian Democrats," said Deputy Assistant Secretary Briggs on April 1, "include some very liberal people. They include some very moderate people. Even the one that is furthest to the right includes individuals who have been described to me by members of the Christian Democratic Party as very liberal ..." Addressing statements by former U.S. Ambassador to El Salvador Robert White that characterized Roberto D'Aubuisson as a "psychopathic killer," current U.S. Ambassador Deane Hilton said of D'Aubuisson, " ... there are people who say he's been dangerous, but he's been a political leader and I think he's behaved very well."[249] The message was clear: although Ambassador Hinton stressed to party leaders in San Salvador the importance of including Christian Democrats in the government the administration was prepared to live with whatever coalition emerged.

The hardest choices will be for the U.S. Congress. As the chances for a negotiated solution recede, the Congress will be asked to appropriate ever higher levels of economic and military aid to a government bent on a military solution to the conflict. "I think the real significance of the Salvadoran election," said Sen. Claiborne Pell on April 1, "is that all the people of that war-torn nation want peace." Perhaps the greatest irony of the 1982 election in El Salvador is that peace seems more distant than ever.

243. Secretary of State Alexander Haig's statement to reporters on elections in El Salvador, quoted in *The New York Times,* March 30, 1982.

244. U.S. Congress Senate Foreign Relations Committee, Hearings on Senate Joint Resolution 144 to Encourage Negotiations for a Settlement of the Conflict in El Salvador, April 1, 1982.

245. Quoted in *The Washington Post*, April 3, 1982.

246. Analysis of the voting results has been compiled from statistics published in *FBIS*, March 31 and April 1 and 2, 1982, and San Salvador's *Diario Latino*, April 1, 1982.

247. See *The Nation*, April 10, 1982.

248. Quoted in *The Washington Post*, April 1, 1982.

249. Quoted in *The Washington Post*, March 30, 1982.

ABOUT THE AUTHOR

Cynthia Arnson is a Latin American specialist and a Visiting Fellow at the Institute for Policy Studies. She has researched and written widely on U.S.-Latin America relations, and U.S. arms sales and military assistance, and is a former legislative aide in the U.S. House of Representatives. She has travelled to Central America and El Salvador several times, and is a regular contributor to "Central America Watch" in *The Nation*. Ms. Arnson is a doctoral candidate at The School of Advanced International Studies of The Johns Hopkins University.